# Joseph

## Dreamer of Dreams

### A BIBLICAL NOVEL

# ELLEN GUNDERSON TRAYLOR

**HARVEST HOUSE PUBLISHERS, INC.**
Eugene, Oregon 97402

## Other Books by Ellen Gunderson Traylor

Song of Abraham
John—Son of Thunder
Mary Magdalene
Noah
Ruth—A Love Story
Jonah
Mark—Eyewitness
Esther—The Story of a Woman Who Saved a Nation

**JOSEPH—DREAMER OF DREAMS**

Copyright © 1989 by Harvest House Publishers, Inc.
Eugene, Oregon 97402

Library of Congress Cataloging-in-Publication Data

Traylor, Ellen Gunderson.
    Joseph / Ellen Gunderson Traylor.
        p.      cm.
    Bibliography:  p.
    ISBN 0-89081-699-9
    1.  Joseph (Son of Jacob)—Fiction.    2. Bible.  O.T.—History of
Biblical events—Fiction.        I. Title.
    PS3570.R357J6 1989
813′.54—dc19                                                          88-7649
                                                                          CIP

**Printed in the United States of America.**

*For My Sons*

*Who have taught me about Brotherhood.*

# Contents

*Behold, how good and how pleasant it is for
brothers to dwell together in unity!*

Psalm 133:1 NASB

# PROLOGUE

The boy crept between the tents of the dark caravan, avoiding the glow of a dozen campfires. The spine of mountains running south from Bethel to Ephrath was capped with frost tonight, and the boy's feet crunched against an icy powder as he sought his mother's tent.

His father, Jacob, had ordered him to spend the night with Bilhah, his mother's maid. "She will care for you," Jacob had insisted. "Your mother cannot do so just now."

Young Joseph had not needed to ask the reason. He understood that Rachel would give birth this very evening. He understood that he could not be with her.

Still, he had awaited this event for years. It had been only a few months since his mother had told him she would have another child. But he had longed for a brother of his very own for as long as he could remember. Even a sister would be better than nothing, he reasoned.

His half brothers, Dan and Naphtali, were no fun. Though they were his father's children by his mother's maid, they looked down on him, considering themselves better than him because they were older.

It mattered not that Rachel was Jacob's beloved and that Bilhah was only a servant. Joseph was scorned because he was the baby and, he knew, because he was Jacob's favorite.

But tonight there would be *another* baby, and another favorite! Joseph would no longer be alone.

When Bilhah had bedded him down in her tent at sunset, Joseph pretended to sleep. He knew she would leave as soon as he did so, for she would be needed in the birthing tent.

Dan and Naphtali snored contentedly outside as Joseph sneaked away. He was glad for this. They surely would have reported his escape, not caring that he fretted over his mother's welfare, or that he yearned to glimpse the newborn.

If he could only make it past the shelters of Leah, Rachel's sister and Jacob's eldest wife, and her handmaid, he might be safe. Once near his mother's tent, he knew no one would turn him away.

As he inched through camp, he considered how often he had known fear. Too many of his ten years had been spent on the run as he and his father's people fled from one threat after another.

Even among the folk of his tribe, Joseph sensed that his safety was often in jeopardy. No one had ever demonstrated that this was true. But he was the eleventh son born to Jacob, and because he was Rachel's, Leah hated him.

So did her children—at least most of them.

The goatshair birthing tent was now visible, pitched at the center of the tribal circle. As he came upon it, he heard cries of anguish from within.

He had heard women in travail before. In a tribe the size of Jacob's, the drama of birth was commonplace. Joseph remembered the bustle of the midwives and the tense expectation in the air whenever a baby was due.

But the sounds coming from his mother's tent tonight were frightening. Her pain was greater than it should be.

Joseph's boyish heart sped as he drew within the tent's shadow. Anxiously he peered through the curl of smoke wafting from the fire outside, but as he leaned around a support pole, studying the fretful scurry of the midwives, he was suddenly pushed face first to the ground.

Rising up on scraped knuckles, he stared into the leering countenance of Simeon, Leah's second son. He was a grown man, eight years older than Joseph and as vicious as a mountain cat.

Joseph crawled to his knees and brushed his dark curls from his forehead. His large black eyes snapping, he challenged: "Leave me be, Simeon! My father is in that tent. He will come after you!"

"*Your* father?" the bully spat, the red of his bushy beard catching firelight. "Always *your* father! Who do you suppose sired *me*? Some *field hand*?"

Tears rose hot in Joseph's eyes, but he restrained them as he stumbled to his feet and, firsts clenched, glared brazenly up at his muscular opponent. Even stretched to his fullest height, he came only to Simeon's chest, and the athletic fellow sneered down upon him with gritted teeth.

"Shouldn't you be asleep, Little One?" Simeon laughed. "It is a full hour since sunset."

"My mother needs me!" the lad cried, trying to push past the human bulwark.

But it was no use. Immediately another enemy emerged from the darkness, Simeon's younger brother Levi, and a scuffle ensued, the two big fellows passing Joseph back and forth between them like a sack of barley chaff.

Such a disturbance was not long ignored, as folk left their fires and their shelters to gather around the tussling trio.

It was Reuben, Leah's eldest, who at last intervened. His commanding voice parting the crowed, he came upon Simeon and Levi like an avenging angel.

"Leave the boy alone!" he commanded—and grasping both of his brothers by the necks, he cast them aside.

Joseph, who lay sprawled like a discarded doll, awkwardly lifted himself from the ground and reached for Reuben's hand.

The rescuer gently raised him up and, with friendly pats, brushed the dust from the lad's tunic.

Joseph studied him with grateful amazement. Reuben could just as easily have joined the tormentors. Though he was not the cruel sort, he could be impetuous. Joseph counted himself fortunate that the volatile young man had taken his side tonight.

"This is what comes of sneaking out at bedtime, Small One," Reuben warned.

The statement was a rebuke, but the tone was kind. Joseph took courage.

"This is what comes of having lions for brothers!" he countered. "Why must they hate me?"

Tears flecked his cheeks, now that he had a sympathizer. But Joseph knew the answer to the question, and Reuben need not reply.

As Simeon and Levi stalked away, uneasy silence descended until Joseph's attention was drawn again to the tent.

"Mother!" he called, responding to another cry of pain issuing on the night air. Darting past Reuben, he forced the crowd aside and pushed through the tent flap.

His sudden entrance jolted Jacob's focus away from his ailing wife, and Joseph confronted a full view of the tent's dark interior.

Never had Rachel looked as she did tonight. Drawn and white, her face was etched with distress. Cold sweat poured from her forehead.

Horrified, Joseph knelt beside the birthing chair, where his mother sat propped against Bilhah's open lap.

The maid was about to chide the boy, but Jacob hushed her.

"Perhaps it is best he is here," the father sighed.

Joseph could have been relieved to hear this. But he did not like the resigned quality in Jacob's voice.

Gazing upon his mother, the boy took her crabbed hand in his and lifted it to his lips.

How often throughout his life had that hand reached for him in tender caress! Now it was unable to reassure him.

And what countless times had he marveled at his mother's ageless face, at the beauty of her violet eyes and golden skin! Now the face was contorted, aged beyond its years in an evening's time.

No word of comfort rose above the panting and the tears from that voice which had sung him to sleep since his earliest memory.

Cradling his head against her swollen belly, Joseph wept. Nor would he be moved until a sudden lurch threw him backward.

Rachel had wrenched with the final throe of travail. For a brief instant, silence filled the room. Then, the shuddering wail of the newborn replaced it.

Joseph's eyes flashed to the baby where it wriggled, wet and red, in the midwife's outstretched hands.

It was a boy! He had a baby brother! He could barely refrain from reaching out to touch it.

But that honor would first be Rachel's, then Jacob's.

As the midwife placed the child on its mother's lap, however, Joseph could see that Rachel was still in anguish.

A fleeting smile touched her lips as the babe nuzzled against her. But just as quickly, the smile vanished, and Rachel pressed herself back against Bilhah, looking as though a searing iron had passed through her.

"Ben Oni!" Rachel cried. "Ben Oni!"

She was naming the child, and the name was not pleasant. "Child of my pain," the words meant. And Rachel clutched the little one to her breast, weeping.

"Mother!" Joseph implored. "What is it?"

But now the woman was still, her head limp against Bilhah's chest, her hands loosening their grip on the squalling infant.

Suddenly Jacob was on his knees, rubbing Rachel's hands and arms, pleading with her to respond.

As Bilhah caught the babe, who moved too freely in its mother's loose embrace, Joseph's heart surged.

"Mother!" he cried again.

But the woman did not reply.

Joseph leapt to his feet, refusing to face the truth. Pushing past his father, he entered the night, tears scalding his cheeks.

Heedless of those who tried to halt him, he raced through camp, toward the frosty fields beyond.

Running blindly into the dark, the boy wept aloud, calling out Jehovah's name.

The oppressive loneliness of his life was suddenly overwhelming. That which he daily endured was now suffocating him.

Where was his father's God when Joseph needed him? Why did he appear to Jacob and not to his young son?

As he reached the top of the ridge, he could hear Jacob calling, pleading for him to return. Yet in mad haste Joseph continued to flee until he was far from the lights of camp, far from the reach of human hands.

Falling to his face, he clutched at the icy ground, and for a long while he lay there, his tears melting the frost in little puddles.

Gradually, memories of a long-ago night pressed through his melancholy—memories of a night when his father had felt equally lonely and afraid.

As he sprawled against the earth's cold bosom, he resisted the demanding recollection. It seemed to offer hope—a hope he feared to embrace.

But the memory was persistent, invading his rebellion, piercing his spirit and his soul....

# PART I
## The Wrestler with God

# 1

Though Joseph was only six years old, it was a night he would clearly remember, a night he would never forget.

It was the night his father wrestled with an angel.

Little Joseph never saw the angel. He never saw Jacob struggle with the great being whose hold was stronger than iron, and who would, before the night was over, permanently cripple the man.

But Joseph saw the difference in Jacob. He saw the limping gait which would forever after be his. And though Joseph was very young, he sensed the maturing of his father's character from that night on.

Joseph had every reason to believe in angels. He had heard of them in stories passed down by Jacob from his father Isaac, and from *his* father Abraham before him. He had never seen one himself. But he knew they were as real as the wind that licked over the Gilead hills or the water which tumbled through the Jordan chasm.

Even before the angel moved against his father, however, the night was marked for memory.

For several days Jacob's caravan had been on the road from Padan-Aram toward Canaan. Joseph was too young to understand all that had transpired in Padan-Aram, the land of his birth. He knew that Jacob and Rachel had not been happy there. He knew that Jacob had not gotten on well with Grandfather Laban, Rachel's father. But this was all he understood.

Much clearer to him was the fear toward which the

caravan traveled as it inched out of Mesopotamia and entered the borders east of Jordan River.

He had heard all his life of Esau, Jacob's notorious elder brother. And he knew that Esau lay in wait to kill his father, once the tribe entered Canaan.

Sometimes he wondered why the family must go to Canaan, if danger lurked there. The country of Grand-father Laban had been a safe place. No one had feared for life or welfare in Padan-Aram.

But just as he had always heard of the red and hairy villain, Esau, so he had always heard of Canaan.

"Promised Land," it was called. Land vouchsafed to Great-grandfather Abraham, Grandfather Isaac, and Father Jacob, by the One True God.

Indeed, more than Esau or Canaan or Jordan River or the breezes of Gilead, Joseph had heard of the One True God.

Every morning of his life, Joseph had witnessed Jacob's early-rising prayers, his burning of sweet incense upon piles of rocks outside their tent home, and his monthly offering of a slaughtered lamb for the sins of the tribe.

He knew that there were other people dwelling nearby who did not believe in the One True God, and who had many other gods besides. But he had been assured since infancy that Jehovah was the only God and that he alone was worthy of honor.

Also, Joseph had been told, this God belonged espe-cially to Abraham, Isaac, and Jacob, for they were his chosen people.

Now this night, when the angel wrestled with Jacob, settled over the caravan like a black shroud. Five days earlier, the enormous tribe had entered Gilead. And five days earlier, Jacob had begun to plot his inevitable meet-ing with Esau.

Full of trepidation, Jacob sent messengers ahead to scout for his enemy, to tell him he wanted peace. When the messengers returned, saying that Esau was headed north with four hundred men, terrible fear gripped the tribe.

Tension rose with each step the caravan took through Gilead. According to Jacob, it must break up once it reached the southern edge of the region, and the people must travel in two divisions as they approached Edom, the land where Esau lived.

Earlier that day, before he wrestled with the angel, Jacob sent droves of sheep, cattle, and goats down the road toward Edom, each drove numbering several dozen animals and manned by half-a-dozen shepherds. Seven droves he sent on before the caravan, and the family camped at sunset beside the ford Jabbok at Gilead's southern border.

When night had fully fallen, the great tribe, composed of Jacob's two wives and two concubines, as well as their many children, servants, and servants' families, settled down to sleep. Joseph would never forget watching as Jacob crept away to his tent, looking distressed indeed, the fear of Esau heavy upon him.

It was the middle of the night, the encampment quiet and dark, when suddenly Jacob reappeared. He threw back the flap to Rachel's shelter, rousing the woman and young Joseph, who slept beside her.

In the light of the smoking lamp suspended from the tent roof, the boy say his father's distraught countenance, and his heart raced fearfully. As he pulled close to Rachel, she took his hand and caressed it reassuringly.

But Papa was evidently afraid—how could Joseph not be?

The boy, eyes wide, listened as Jacob gave instructions. "Wife," he began, "I have not been sleeping tonight. The power of God is in this place. Do you feel it?"

Rachel replied nothing, always awed by her husband's intimacy with the Almighty. Shaking her head, she admitted she had no such sense of things.

"I did not tell you," he went on, pacing the room, "but a few days ago I saw the hosts of the Lord encamped about us. The hills were full of them! Bright as sun! Did you not see them?"

Joseph knew "the hosts of the Lord" was another term for angels, and he listened intently.

"No, husband," Rachel answered. "I saw nothing."

"They met me on the road. Surely you saw!"

But Rachel only lowered her eyes.

"So be it," Jacob muttered, obviously disappointed. "But I know the Lord is in this place. I must seek him! Help me rouse the camp. All of you are to cross Jabbok while it is yet dark."

Rachel did not understand. "Why, my lord?" she implored. "Can we not wait with you?"

Jacob could not explain. He only knew that he must be alone, for the Lord would not come to him while he was in company.

Urgently he pressed his command. "Up, Rachel! Take the lad and help me wake the others. We have only a short while before morning."

Certain things about Jacob's character had already been imprinted upon Joseph's young mind. His father was very changeable: sometimes, like now, forceful and commanding; other times, betraying cowardice and uncertainty.

Had Joseph been older, these discrepancies might have caused him to question what Jacob said. He might have doubted the man's visions; he might have doubted the reality of angels altogether.

But the child loved his father passionately. If Jacob said they must be going, Joseph would cooperate.

Jumping up, he ran to a corner of the tent where a satchel was kept, his satchel for carrying toys and valuables dear to his heart. It was full, as he had picked up his possessions before bedtime, and he proudly set it beside the door.

"So, Little One is ready!" Jacob observed, smiling broadly.

Preoccupied, Jacob had barely noticed the child when he had entered the tent. But he beamed now with pride at the handsome lad who so resembled himself.

Calling Joseph, he reached for him, and the boy eagerly rushed into his strong arms.

"Help your mother," Jacob said fondly, his dark eyes mirroring his son's.

With that, the man left, summoning his servants to load the wagons.

Rachel, who was never prepared for her husband's swift alterations, tried not to reveal, by expression or word, the weariness she felt.

Brushing her long black tresses back from a too-pale face, she sighed.

She would much prefer to sleep until morning.

# 2

Joseph huddled between rough sacks of winnowed grain in the back of Leah's jolting wagon. Rachel had prevailed upon her sister to keep the lad in the cart where Leah's daughter, Dinah, was hidden, while she and her handmaid loaded their own supplies. Now he peered out from the protective tarp, watching as Gilead retreated in the night.

Haughty Leah had, in her typical manner, scorned Rachel's request, taking opportunity to gloat over the pleasures of having many children.

"Too bad Joseph has no brothers or sisters of his own to cozy up with," she huffed. "You would do Jacob a service to give him another son."

Rachel's face burned, showing more color than it had in recent weeks. But, nodding, she indulged her jealous sister. For she knew it *was* only jealousy that prompted the cruel remark.

Leah hated Rachel. She hated her because Jacob loved her. And because she knew that Jacob never would have been her own husband, had Father Laban not insisted on it.

It seemed to make no difference that Leah had given Jacob six sons and a daughter, or that her handmaid, Zilpah, had blessed him with two sons more. Though Jacob was justly proud of all his children, Rachel, who had borne him only one heir, held his heart in an unyielding knot of love.

Could Leah help it that she was not as beautiful as her younger sister? Mousy-haired and wan, she had never been smooth-complected or ruby-lipped like Rachel. Could she help it that her vision was weak, so that she could not do the fine needlework for which Rachel was renowned, or that her dull brown eyes did not dance with lavender lights like Rachel's?

Leah was at least a good cook. One did not need perfect vision for that. And Leah was the elder. Surely she deserved preference for that reason, if no other.

Besides, of late Rachel was pale-skinned, the blossom gone from her cheeks. Could not Jacob see the alteration? Was not Leah the stronger of the two?

She would never understand Jacob. From the moment he had shown up in Laban's camp, on the run from Canaan and the threats of Esau, she had been smitten with him. Though her sight had been poor since childhood, she was not completely blind to the lithe and strapping handsomeness of her cousin from the west.

He, on the other hand, had not given Leah a second look.

Jacob had first laid eyes on Rachel, and from that instant his soul belonged to the younger sister.

Over and over, Leah had chided herself for not being in the field the day Jacob arrived. Rachel was tending sheep that afternoon, something the elder girl scorned. Smelly, despicable creatures they were, and whenever possible, she passed the task to Rachel.

But Leah should have been with the sheep the day Jacob came. Perhaps if he had seen her first he would have fallen in love with her, and Rachel would not have moved him as she did.

Thus did Leah comfort herself. Thus did she lie to herself.

Year in and year out she dreamed that the next son she bore would win Jacob's heart from Rachel's grip. To this day, it had not happened. But, in time...

As Joseph hid this night in the covered grain-cart, his half sister, Dinah, nestled close. Dinah was nearest to him in age of all Jacob's children, and despite her mother's objections, she loved the boy dearly.

His sole playmate, she was only two years his senior. But since she was his only female sibling, she enjoyed mothering him at every opportunity.

The wagon rocked against the brook's bottom as the caravan forded the Jabbok River in the dark. Father Jacob was somewhere in the night beyond, shouting commands as loudly as he dared, trying to hasten the train to a safe stopping place.

No one but he understood why the caravan could not wait to pass over in the morning. Only Jacob knew with certainty that he must be alone in Gilead with the Lord.

Dinah pulled Joseph's head to her shoulder, crooning a soft lullaby in his ear. But the child was too old for this, and asserting his masculinity, he pulled away.

Joseph wanted to see where they were going. He wanted to be riding with his father, upon his father's horse.

Reaching for the wagon's back rail, he peered again from beneath the tarp at the long caravan behind.

Just as he did so, two of his half brothers rode up, their horses splashing effortlessly through the cold stream. Though the riders were only teenagers, they were larger than life to Joseph, who held them in high esteem. For Reuben and Judah were generally kind to the youngster.

When the two horsemen caught sight of Joseph's round face and rounder eyes gleaming beneath the moonlit tarp, they laughed, nodding to him. And when Reuben winked congenially, the boy blushed with admiration.

"Where is Papa?" he called. "Have you seen my Papa?"

But already the brothers had passed, their powerful steeds leaving a glistening wake. The only reply Joseph would receive came from two others, following on their trail.

"This son of a second wife calls for his Papa!" a mocking voice announced.

And another scoffed, "You don't suppose he means Jacob? Why I thought Jacob was *your* Papa, Simeon."

"And *yours*, Levi!" the first replied.

Joseph sensed their sarcasm and felt the rejection keenly.

Dinah yanked on the boy's tunic, but he refused to rejoin her, staring after Simeon and Levi with sad eyes.

Reading his dejection, the girl tried to console him. "They are fools!" she whispered, still clutching at his garment. "Never mind those two."

The lad's lower lip jutted in an offended pout. Soon a salty tear slipped down his cheek.

"Let me go!" he cried. "I want Papa!"

At last the caravan reached the south shore and soon a silty dust rose from the damp wheels. Somehow through hazy starlight, the boy spied his father.

Jacob had seen the caravan safely over and waited now on a knoll of the brook's border. Tall and dark against the sky, he sat astride his horse, and Joseph wondered why he did not join them.

When Rachel came looking for her child amidst the grain sacks, Joseph climbed out eagerly. "I want to go to Papa!" he called, directing her attention to the distant figure on the rise.

"Hush, son," Rachel soothed. "He cannot come just now."

"Why?" the lad pleaded. "Is he afraid?"

Flashes of the legendary Esau gripped his imagination, conjuring visions of monsters and assassins.

"Your Papa is never afraid," Rachel whispered.

But Joseph knew better.

"He runs from fighting Esau," the youngster muttered.

Rachel studied her perceptive boy with wonder. Shaking her head, she spoke a mystery.

"It is not Esau whom your Papa must fight tonight. It is the Lord."

The boy absorbed the words in quiet awe. Clutching his mother's skirt, he shivered, still entranced by the figure on the hill.

Suddenly Jacob turned to leave, guiding his mount back into the water. A sheen of moonlight glinted across the waves where the horse's strong legs broke the eddies, and the man sat erect in the saddle.

That moment, Joseph was prouder of his father than he had ever been. For whatever it was that called him back to Gilead, Jacob dared to face it.

# 3

Like the glint off a giant's spear, morning burst upon the caravan.

Joseph, having rested fitfully all night, crawled out from his mother's tent and rubbed his bleary eyes in the glaring sun.

The great train had set up camp close to the brook, but because Rachel's and Leah's tents were at the center of the encircling tribe, Joseph could not see the place where his father had departed.

Somehow he knew Jacob would be returning early from whatever had faced him in Gilead. Scrambling between the wagons, he found the edge of camp before any adult awoke to find him gone, and when he gained the brook's shore, he peered across the undulating hills on the far side.

Within moments his eager expectation was rewarded. The sight of his father emerging from a crease of the northern slopes provoked a cry of delight.

But presently his enthusiasm was dampened as Jacob appeared to slump in his horse's saddle.

"Papa! Papa!" the boy called until the caravan was roused, and men and women joined him on shore.

The closer the rider came, the more evident was his sorry condition. In the blaring sunlight, sweat streaked his body. Beneath a layer of dirt, the scrapes and bruises on his torso, arms, and legs throbbed.

Horrified, Joseph stood dangerously close to the water's edge, trying to reach across. In an instant he was grasped from behind, hoisted to someone's shoulders and scolded without mercy.

It was Reuben who held him, Reuben who scolded him. But Joseph kicked his heels into the tall fellow's breast.

"Enough, Little One!" the elder snarled, grasping his ankles. "See what a good view you have from up there! Jacob is nearly here now."

Leah, her eyes snapping, came near to Reuben, ready to reprimand him for associating so closely with the lad. But with a look, he silenced her.

Jacob had reached the southern shore and, dismounting, he staggered, holding onto the saddle for support.

A gasp went up from the crowd, and those nearest rushed to help him.

But soon they were pushed aside as Rachel forced her way through to her husband.

"Jacob, what is it?" she cried, seeing how he limped upon one leg. "What has happened to you?"

Bending over, she probed his leg with deft hands, seeking a broken or disjointed bone.

"Not there!" he grimaced as she reached toward the backside of his thigh. "Do not touch me there! And do not call me 'Jacob,' for the Almighty has called me 'Israel.'"

This was spoken with such authority that the woman jolted upright, staring into the man's face as into the face of a stranger.

Israel. "Wrestler with God," the name implied. Joseph remembered how his mother had said Papa must fight with the Lord, and clutching Reuben closer, he studied Jacob with wonder.

The patriarch gave no further explanation, only passing through the crowd until he came to the center of the caravan.

Snapping his fingers, he called for a bucket of water and began washing himself in the presence of the people.

Gingerly he cleansed his own wounds, all the while avoiding the tender spot beneath his hip.

His tunic, which hung in shreds upon his naked body, must be removed, and Jacob, disregarding public exposure, lifted it over his head, cast it aside, and stood for all to see covered only by his loincloth.

When he called for a clean garment, Leah ran to her supply cart, unfurled a freshly laundered tunic, and brought it to him.

Almost in ritual did Jacob don the spotless garb. When he pulled it over his tall form, he raised his eyes toward heaven in private communion.

The crowd, riveted by his strange behavior and by the mystery of his struggle in the wilderness, watched in breathless suspense.

For a long time he stood thus, head back, eyes closed, until the quiet of the hills was broken. Somewhere beyond the valley of the Jabbok, from across the southland, the sound of a tramping horde invaded the tranquil moment.

On the instant, Jacob ceased his prayers. With a stalwart stride, he passed toward the highlands hemming the caravan's southern rim.

Every heart in the company surged with fear. They knew it was Esau who advanced upon them—Esau with his army of four hundred.

Before the dust-raising horsemen appeared on the barren hills, Jacob began shouting orders.

"Each man to arms!" he cried. "Advance to the front, but keep your weapons in their sheaths!"

The order was, on the surface, contradictory. But to this point Jacob had let Esau know that he intended peace. The sight of bared swords and poised arrows would indicate the contrary.

Louder and louder came the sound of the troops, billows of fine silt wafting skyward from their marching feet, lingering on the warm currents above the rise and signaling the company's ascent toward the Jabbok.

Sweat streaked the faces of Jacob's servants and shepherds, who, though they had been trained for battle, had no experience with it. In awkward bands they arranged themselves along the edge of the caravan, ready to kneel behind the carts, ready to draw their primitive staves and heavy knives.

With amazing coolness, Jacob called to his womenfolk, ordering his maids and their children to stay nearest the caravan, while his wives and concubines gathered near the brook.

"Bilhah and Zilpah!" he shouted. "Leave room for Leah and her children behind you!"

Readily the women complied, trying to keep their anxieties under control.

As they arranged themselves according to his instruction, he turned his attention to Rachel and Joseph. In that moment he revealed, as never before, the exact priorities of his heart.

"Wife," he called, "take the final station! And keep Little One with you at all times!"

Leah did not notice this interchange. She was distracted by her four eldest sons, who bitterly resented Jacob's restraint, and who desired to be in the forefront with the men.

But Dinah frantically tugged on her mother's skirts, pointing to Joseph.

"May I stay with my brother?" she pleaded. "It is safest where he and his mother are."

The elder woman flashed angry eyes on Rachel and on her husband. Never had she hated her sister as she did just now, and never had she felt such antipathy for the man she craved.

Scooping Dinah into her arms, she ran for the privacy of her canopied wagon, where she would stay, hidden and heartsick, until the crisis was over.

As for the rest of the company, all eyes were on the patriarch as he faced the southern hills.

Emerging along the horizon were the four hundred soldiers, and leading them, a ruddy commander. Esau, whose thick red beard and heavy turban lent him a fearsome aspect, rode a big-boned mount. Black and glistening, the horse's studded saddle and burnished harnesswork befitted the legendary image of its master.

Jacob's men flinched at the sight. For weeks, they had dreaded this moment, their imaginations piqued by the tales that had long circulated in Padan-Aram of this son of Isaac and his vendetta against the younger brother.

Wet palms slipped against the handles of their swords and coveted the feel of the bow. How the men longed to break with Jacob's order, to draw their weapons and fell Esau where he stood!

But it was Jacob who would make the first move. And his move would be peaceable.

Confronting the man who watched from the mountain, the patriarch began a slow advance up the rise that hemmed Jabbok Vale.

As he did so, his would-be soldiers poised their hands to grasp their weapons. But their commander would not indulge them.

It was with the attitude of a servant that Jacob approached his brother, his limping gait evincing pain with each step. To the amazement of his troops, he began to bow, over and over, as he walked up the hill toward Esau. Nor was this a cursory gesture. Six times he performed the obeisance—stopping in his tracks, falling to his knees, and with arms outstretched along the ground, touching his black-bearded face to the earth.

That scene would be indelibly imprinted upon the mind of Joseph. He had long sensed Jacob's fear of this very encounter; he had witnessed his restless nights and the growing agitation of his spirit as they had come near the land of Esau. But Jacob's behavior this day, though

self-effacing, bore no hint of cowardice or helpless sur-
render. The patriarch manifested strength of purpose,
steadfastly pursuing the meeting even as he declared his
humility.

The boy, staying close to Rachel, observed the drama
with wonder. He did not comprehend why Esau wished
to kill Jacob, nor why his father had run from the land of
Canaan years ago. But he did know that Uncle Esau could
take Jacob's life at any moment.

For the younger brother was no longer running. Jacob
had come home, and he hid behind no army, no weapon
of his own. He was offering himself as a sacrifice, appealing to whatever goodwill Esau might possess, and ready
to die rather than run again.

As he approached the enemy, the crowd's attention
shifted to Esau, who sat unmoving, watching his brother
with stormy eyes.

Not only were years of Jacob's personal history about
to be resolved, but the fate of the entire tribe hinged on
Esau's response—the fate of innocent hundreds who had
followed the younger patriarch out from Padan-Aram.

To this point, the company from the east had been
awed by their leader's bravery. However, the seventh time
Jacob bowed himself to the ground, he was nearly within
the shadow of Esau's horse. The elder brother had the
right, at that juncture, to climb down from his steed,
placing his foot directly upon Jacob's neck. Should he
choose to do so, he would in fact be conqueror of Jacob
and all his people—a conqueror without a war.

Never had the Jacobites dreamed their patriarch would
stoop so low! Had he brought them out from their homeland only to hand them into slavery? Incredulous, they
witnessed his symbolic submission, and a rush of angry
whispers filled the vale.

For a long, anxious moment, Esau studied his prostrate brother. It seemed a lifetime since he had last laid

eyes on the prodigal—a lifetime of festering hatred and desire for revenge.

When Jacob had slunk away from Canaan, he had been a desperate character, poor as an alms seeker, possessing nothing but his guilt and the clothes on his back. Now here he came, returning from his hideaway, chieftain of a mighty tribe, leader of a fabulous caravan.

When the first bevy of cattle and presents had arrived on the southbound highway, brought by peace-seeking messengers, Esau had been amazed at his brother's apparent success in the land of Uncle Laban. But he despised the placating gesture, and his longing for vengeance had only been piqued by Jacob's show of wealth, his belated attempt at appeasement.

Now as he gazed down upon the penitent, his heart was a muddle of conflict. Part of him yearned to squash the fellow into the dirt. It would be so easy to do so. Another part seethed with resentment at the ease of such conquest, for Jacob had effectively taken the luxury of violence from his sword-hungry hand.

There was a nobler motivation, however, which was stirred by Jacob's humble homecoming. It was brotherhood, the kind that had resisted all attempts to kill itself.

For Jacob was bone of his bone, flesh of his flesh—his twin, born at the same hour, born in tandem with him, grasping his heel (so the legend went) as Esau declared his supremacy, his right to primogeniture.

From that moment, the secondborn was called Jacob, "the supplanter," and so he had proven himself to be—fighting and scratching for equality, and ultimately, by connivery and deceit, winning the birthright itself.

But at this instant, as Esau observed Jacob's willingness to make amends, none of that seemed to matter.

Suddenly, in a breath, the heart of the elder melted, and the past was absolved. Barely understanding his own actions, Esau leapt to the ground and ran the short distance between them, bending over and grasping Jacob by the shoulders.

The runaway lifted his head, staring into Esau's face in bewildered amazement. What he saw there astonished him: tears streamed down Esau's cheeks, trickling into his crimson beard as he lifted his brother from the dirt. Embracing Jacob, Esau fell on his neck and kissed him, and together the men wept.

Drawing back, Esau looked his long-lost brother up and down, and grasped him close again and again, letting the tears flow.

After this catharsis of revelry, Esau studied the great multitude waiting on the plain below.

"Who are these with you?" he inquired.

Jacob could hardly speak, absorbed as he was in the incredible turnabout.

"The children whom God has graciously given me," he at last replied, beaming with pride.

Wheeling around he motioned to the throng and called for his wives and young ones to come forward.

Bilhah and Zilpah, nearest the front, complied first, trailed by their reticent sons: Dan, Naphtali, Gad, and Asher. Lingering at the foot of the hill, they bowed themselves.

Next came Leah, who by now had seen the necessity of emerging from her cart, obeying her husband in begrudging silence.

Her sons were no more willing to condescend than she. Hotheaded and strong-willed, all six of them resisted this twist of events, but one by one they fell in line behind their mother in order of their age: Reuben, Simeon, Levi, Judah, Issachar, and Zebulun.

Stiffnecked, the lads bowed before their uncle, wishing his heart had not changed before them, wishing he had chosen war.

Dinah, clinging to Leah's skirts, peered back at Joseph, wondering what he thought. But he paid her no mind.

Alone among his brothers, Joseph was eager to meet the amazing Esau.

At last, Jacob called for Rachel, his expression soft, his voice full of love.

"This is my wife," he introduced her, "and this is Joseph, my youngest."

Esau could not have missed the tenderness in his brother's tone. Obviously Rachel held his heart, and Joseph, though least of the brethren, was foremost in his father's estimation.

Nor could the other people in Jacob's company miss the intimation. Even Reuben, who loved the boy, felt the prick of jealousy, and his body grew rigid. With mixed emotions, he watched as his young brother strode boldly up to Esau, bowing to the ground just as Jacob had done.

Esau, a lump in his throat, gazed on the lad, and Joseph lifted his round face to the "villain" whose very name had always filled the child with horror.

Leaning down, Esau held out his hairy arms, and without hesitating, Joseph ran to him. Raised up on the man's broad shoulders, he saw the great tribe from the "enemy's" perspective.

Though Jacob had every right to be proud of his company, it did not compare to the trained army at Esau's back. Joseph knew that Esau could have wiped out his people, and he keenly perceived the man's merciful kindness.

"Brother," Esau was speaking again, "what was the meaning of all the gifts you sent before you?"

Jacob looked at the ground. "They were to find grace in the sight of my lord," he replied.

"But I have enough, my brother," Esau said, smiling. "Keep your possessions."

Jacob shook his head. "No, I beg of you; if I have found grace in your sight, receive my gift. For I have seen your face, and it is like the face of God. You have forgiven me.

Now please take my gift, for it is the gift of the Lord unto
your servant."

Joseph, who clung to Esau's neck, felt him tremble as
he at last relented, accepting Jacob's love and loving him
in return.

In that instant the lad knew that not only had Jacob
changed during the struggle of the night, but that change
had also altered the heart of Esau.

Whatever had transpired in the hills of Gilead had
indeed been supernatural. Joseph would always wish he
had seen the encounter firsthand.

# 4

For four years Jacob and his people dwelt on the east side of the Jordan River. And for four years, Joseph pondered the mystery of his father's fight in Gilead.

Not once in all that time did he speak with Jacob about the incident. Perhaps he felt the topic too holy to pursue. Perhaps he feared it.

When he was ten years old, the great tribe moved across the Jordan into the legendary region of Canaan, into the Promised Land where Abraham and Isaac had dwelt. With that move, Joseph hungered even more after spiritual things. He longed to understand the mystery of his people and the tales of the elders.

Indeed, Grandfather Isaac still lived there. Though his dwelling place was at the Oaks of Mamre, in Hebron—much farther to the south than the place where Jacob settled—Joseph hoped to one day meet the venerable fellow. As the boy grew toward manhood, so did his curiosity regarding Isaac's God.

After the tribe made its entrance into Canaan, Jacob selected a site near Shalem to pitch his tent.

Shalem, nestled in the pleasant hill country twenty miles west of the Jordan, was the headquarters of Hamor, a Hivite, and his eldest son. In fact, the region around Shalem was named for the son, Shechem, who was considered prince of the region.

The Hivites were a violent brood, lovers of war and jealous territorialists. But then so were most Canaanites, and Jacob knew that diplomacy would be required wherever his tribe settled.

Joseph sat one noon in the sunny patch outside his mother's tent. Across the narrow common that ran between the dwellings of Jacob's wives he watched as Leah brushed out his sister Dinah's auburn hair.

The girl had persuaded her mother to let her go into town to sell some of their honey cakes at market.

Leah had come upon an abandoned hive in a hollow tree trunk the day before, and Dinah had helped her knead and bake the succulent yeast dough which was sweetened to a mouth-watering confection. All morning the aroma of rising dough and browning loaves had filled the vale where the caravan rested. One by one Dinah had glazed the rolls with cinnamon and honey and had carefully wrapped them in oilcloth. They were stacked now in a satchel at her feet, waiting to be carried to Shalem's bazaar.

Joseph was not too young to realize how pretty his sister was. Eagerly he waited while she stood and turned about for her mother's inspection, her flowing gown conforming to her willowy legs as she twirled.

He would be very proud to accompany Dinah to Shalem. And he was thrilled that the girl had persuaded Leah to let him do so. No one else was available to be her escort, as all the older brothers were off in the high fields, tending Jacob's herds.

For days, Dinah had fretted over the desire to go to market, to meet the girls of the town and make some friends. Hers was a lonely existence, sole daughter among eleven sons. Since Jacob had rented Hamor's campsite for the entire season, she knew she would have time, for once, to form relationships.

Joseph, likewise, was lonely. Though there were playmates among the servants' children, he, like Dinah, was the child of the tribal elder. Neither of them was very free to mingle with the lower class.

For Joseph, however, loneliness went beyond this. This morning his elder brothers had brushed him off when he requested to go with them into the hills.

Always he was "Little One." More than this, he was "Rachel's son," and he sensed increasingly that he had inherited the same jealous treatment his mother had always endured at Leah's hands.

The sons of Bilhah, Rachel's maid, were less resentful of Joseph than were the others. But even these, Dan and Naphtali, often snubbed him, knowing that he was Jacob's favorite.

Perhaps, Joseph thought, he would meet some youths of his own age and class in Shalem. Anticipating a delightful afternoon, he was impatient for Dinah to be ready.

Although Joseph related to his sister's isolation, one thing lately gave him great enthusiasm for the future. No one had told him, but he knew that his mother was pregnant. And he trusted with all his heart that she would present him with a brother.

Just now, Rachel emerged from her tent and passed before him in the sunlight. With boyish curiosity Joseph observed how her long tunic stretched more snugly than usual over her abdomen. And he noticed that her lap string was riding higher on her belly.

He also knew, based on his observations of other ladies in the tribe, that it would yet be several months before she bore the child. Eagerly he contemplated the event, running his tongue over his lips as the idea tantalized him.

At last Dinah joined him, her beauty session at an end. Following his gaze across the courtyard, she softly rebuked him. "It isn't nice to stare. You could embarrass your mother."

Joseph jolted, and receiving the correction, blushed violently. "I . . . I didn't mean . . ." he stammered.

"Come," the girl laughed, tossing her red-brown curls as she turned on her heel. "Time to go."

Joseph leapt to his feet and ran to catch up with her. Offering to carry Dinah's satchel, he gloated, "Mama is going to have a baby!"

Dinah giggled. "Hush," she warned. "Such things should not be spoken until your mother says so."

But Joseph was heedless. Matching Dinah's stride, he beamed proudly, as though he could somehow take credit for his good fortune.

\* \* \*

The marketplace of Shalem was crowded with afternoon shoppers when Joseph and Dinah arrived.

With a light step, the daughter of Jacob sauntered through the aisles, admiring the produce, the pottery, and the dry goods arrayed in colorful rows all about.

Only moments after entering the bazaar, Dinah sold her honey loaves. Though she was certain she must be a natural hawker after striking an ample deal on her first try, Joseph was not so sure it was business savvy that had brought her price.

It had not escaped his notice that the old codger she dealt with seemed to be swayed as much by her endearing charms as by the quality of her wares. Nodding his head enthusiastically, his little goatee bobbing and his pea-black eyes twinkling, he had purchased her entire satchel-load with hardly a quibble.

In fact, Joseph found his protective hackles rising as he accompanied his sister through the market's narrow walkways. For all about were men, old and young, observing the maiden with undisguised admiration.

Dinah, who seemed oblivious to the onlookers' unabashed stares, had but one thing in mind now that she had sold her baked goods: She had come to market to meet girls her own age. She searched the booths and the klatches of customers, hoping to find companions.

At last she spotted a group of young ladies gathered about the stall of a fabric vendor, and she eagerly turned to Joseph.

"Now, you are my escort," she reminded him. "You must introduce me."

"Me?" Joseph objected. "Not for a bag of silver! I'll not join any gaggle of girls! Let go!" he barked, jerking his sleeve from her grasp.

"Hush!" she ordered, her face scarlet. "They'll hear you."

But it seemed they had already heard, and they watched the awkward interchange with muted laughter.

"Now you've done it!" Dinah sighed, her lip jutted in a pout. "I'll never make friends here!"

Putting her hands to her tear-streaked face, she headed for a quiet alcove behind the town fountain. Joseph, unprepared for this reaction, stood dejected in the midst of the bustling market.

When he saw that the girls at the fabric stall twittered hilariously, he turned with humiliation to join his sister.

By the time he reached her, however, someone else had come to her rescue. Joseph stopped in his tracks as a strapping fellow, dressed in princely finery, approached Dinah upon a tall white steed.

The son of Jacob was not the only one to be amazed at the sudden appearance of this character. Young ladies throughout the marketplace turned to gaze upon the stately fellow, whispering his name and pointing. For Prince Shechem, son of Hamor, lord of the region, did not often mingle with commoners.

As Joseph came upon his sister, cloistered behind the fountain, the man had already dismounted and bent over the maiden as though he knew her.

Stunned, Joseph did not know how to approach the prince.

For royalty he was—tall and handsome, his glistening black beard set off against a tunic of rose-colored satin.

Upon his head was a sequined turban, and draped about his broad shoulders was a velvet cloak, wine-hued and embroidered in silver.

Nevertheless, Joseph did not appreciate the man's familiar gesture. Standing at the corner of the alcove, he listened to the fellow's smooth talk and tender words as he tried to comfort the girl.

"Sir," Joseph interrupted, clearing his throat, "that is *my* sister. You would do well to leave her alone!"

Dinah, who by now had turned to face the stranger, seemed highly impressed by the man. Glaring at Joseph, she warned him with a look to keep his peace.

Joseph, however, would not be dissuaded. Young though he was, and small, he was still her escort, and he would not be deterred from his protective duty.

The prince greeted the interruption with a smile, his white teeth shining in his moustached face.

"This is *my* city," he countered, as though speaking to the lad took more condescension than he was used to. "I do not like to see a maiden weeping within these gates."

Joseph, put off by his silky manner, his costly raiment, and perfectly crimped coiffure, was momentarily struck dumb. But lifting his chin, he argued, "We are children of Jacob the Hebrew, who rents land from your father. You would do well to keep our goodwill!"

Shechem rolled his eyes, looking to the hills as though they bored him. He was about to fling out an epithet regarding the bedouin lifestyle, but caught himself as he considered Dinah's feelings. Not wishing to offend the object of his desire, he recast his approach.

"Please give your father my regards," he said, bowing to Joseph. Then, turning to Dinah, he took her hand and kissed it softly. "You and I, dear lady, shall meet again."

With this he remounted his horse, and hailing the girl, exited through the market gate.

Dinah stood mute with wondering adoration.

But her brother's skin crawled. He suspected the man meant just what he said: He and Dinah would meet again. The prospect did not sit well with Joseph.

# 5

Joseph lurched awake. It was the middle of the night, he knew, by the slant of the moon's rays entering his mother's tent.

Someone stood silhouetted in the doorway, and as his pulse raced, he realized it was Dinah.

He sat up in bed, ready to call her name, but she hushed him. "You'll wake Rachel," she said. "Come out here."

Dinah's voice was strained and urgent. When Joseph joined her on the common, he saw that she stood hunched and shaking in the shadows.

"What is it?" he whispered. "Are you all right?"

The girl shuddered. "Tell no one," she implored as she pulled him toward the grove of oak trees that sheltered the camp. "You must promise to tell no one."

"Tell what?" the boy puzzled.

"I left Leah's tent this evening. I could not sleep for thinking of Prince Shechem."

Joseph rolled his eyes, but Dinah shook her head. "This is important, Little One," she insisted. Then, studying her own quivering hands, she groaned, "I have been defiled. Do not hate me."

The lad had heard the term before. He knew what "defiled" meant. But he could not couple the idea with his sister.

"I do not understand," he sighed.

Dinah, surveying his innocent face, began to sob, and she led him to a fallen log, where they sat together.

"I wandered out from camp tonight," she confessed, her chest heaving. "Farther out than I should have gone. Everyone was asleep. The prince must have been waiting for me. I do not know how he knew . . . but he found me in the vale. And . . ."

Her voice broke, and she choked back the longing to cry aloud.

Quickly the scenario flashed through Joseph's mind. "The swine!" he spat, leaping to his feet. "I shall kill him!"

His fist clenched, he looked about frantically, as if seeking a weapon with which to wreak revenge. Bending down, he ripped one of the dry roots off the fallen tree and lunged through the darkness, wielding it like a battle-ax.

"I will tell Jacob!" he declared. "You return to your mother!"

With this, he was off.

"I begged you not to tell! You mustn't tell, Joseph!" Dinah called.

Running after him, she caught him about the waist, pulling him to the ground.

Though the girl had been badly shaken, she was still stronger than her little brother. Staring him full in the face as she wrestled him into submission, she pleaded, "Hear me. Shechem says he loves me. He says he wishes to marry me. Perhaps he is not so evil!"

Incredulous, Joseph lay stone still, his thoughts a blur.

"Are you lunatic?" he muttered, his teeth gritted. Then with an accusing tone, he asked, "*Did* he force you, or didn't he?"

Dinah drew back, appalled at the intimation. "Why . . . why . . ." she faltered, "what do you take me for?"

"*Did* he force you," Joseph challenged, "or did you . . ."

At this, Dinah's eyes flashed, and slapping her brother across the cheek, she rose, running deep into the woods.

"Of course he forced you!" Joseph shouted after her.

Scrambling to his feet he leapt like a deer through the oak vale, disappearing toward Jacob's tent.

Once Joseph was out of sight, Dinah fell to her knees, alone and desolate. Suddenly she knew not who she was. She could not be certain of her role in what had transpired. Was she a victim, or had she invited Shechem's advances?

Impressions and distortions from the interlude tormented her: the fear, the guilt, the pleasure.

And now a searing pain shot up from her groin, and she rocked to and fro, her heart and body in conflict.

She knew not whether to love Shechem or hate him. She knew nothing about life whatsoever.

* * *

Father Jacob sat in the shadow of the oaks outside his tent door. Between the fingers of his right hand he twirled a foxtail reed, twisting it in hypnotic circles as he gazed across the plain of the Hivites.

He had not spoken to anyone all morning. He had not pursued his daily chores, nor even communed with Rachel.

Joseph, who milked one of his mother's cows, observed Jacob from across the common, wondering what ran through his mind.

Ever since he had relayed the news of Dinah's defilement, he had been amazed at Jacob's composure. When he had entered the man's tent before dawn, waking him with the story, the patriarch had only drawn up rigid on his sleeping mat, and after a long moment, had replied, "You have done well, Joseph. Go to bed."

All day the man had sat alone outside his door, obviously deep in thought, watching the plain as though he expected someone. Joseph might have concluded that he awaited the arrival of the ten elder sons, who had been away in the shepherd fields. But the fields they worked were behind the camp, in the hills, and not down in Shalem Vale, which Jacob faced.

Now and then Joseph noticed a smug look cross Jacob's features. What he could be plotting, or how he could take any pleasure from his daughter's pain, the lad could not imagine.

But mostly the man just sat there, unmoving, silent; his countenance brooding and sullen.

When, upon a rare occasion, his eyes left the plain, they traveled to the great stone altar he had erected upon first arriving here. As though he sought guidance, he would linger over the pedestal, communing with his God.

Joseph rested his head against the cow's warm flank, his heart aching for both Dinah and Jacob. So long had the patriarch held his peace that it came as a great surprise when he suddenly spoke aloud.

"Does she love him?" he asked.

The boy, not certain his father addressed him, rose and wiped his milk-stained hands upon his cloak.

"What, sir?" he said.

"Your sister—does she love this man?"

"How should I know?" Joseph shrugged, tracing his toe through the dirt.

"You should know because she came to you in her hour of need," Jacob reasoned, disliking the lad's insolent tone.

Joseph looked up sheepishly. "I suppose she thinks she loves him," he admitted. "But . . . what can *she* know?"

At this, Jacob rebuked him sharply. "A man of God will respect his ladies!" he commanded. "Do not speak disparagingly of your sister!"

The lad received this like a cold slap. "Yes, sir," he whispered.

Jacob now returned to his silence, twirling the reed around and around. At last he inquired, "Did she say how he treated her? Did he speak his heart to Dinah?"

Joseph, increasingly uneasy with the topic, wished his father would ask these things of the girl, and not of himself. But Dinah had hidden all day in Leah's tent, and Jacob, taking pity, had let her do so.

"She says he spoke tenderly to her—that he was kind—and that he..."

"Yes?" Jacob prodded.

"...that he wishes to marry her."

This last, Joseph hated to acknowledge. As he feared, it seemed to please Jacob.

"I have heard good things of Shechem," the patriarch recalled. "Better things of him than of his father..."

"Papa, you cannot think... But Papa, Shechem defiled my sister!"

Jacob heard this objection, but made no reply. He knew that Joseph saw no redeeming potential in the evil wrought against the girl. But the patriarch would not expound the possibilities just now.

The elder brothers, returning from the fields, could be heard descending the hill behind. Jacob must turn his attention to them and must break the news of their sister's shame.

# 6

Jacob's elder sons paced the slope before his tent, breathing out vendettas against Shechem and Hamor.

Back and forth they stalked, Simeon raving, Levi pounding his fist against his thigh, Reuben and Judah plotting revenge.

Gad and Asher sat muttering together, while Issachar and Zebulun, Dinah's closest brothers, seethed to avenge the girl's honor.

Over and over Jacob sought to temper their impetuous spirits.

"Consider Dinah's feelings as well as her reputation!" he warned. "Do you know her heart or the heart of this Shechem?"

"We know an evil deed when we hear of one!" Simeon declared. "Surely you do not defend the Canaanite! Such a thing as he has done ought not to be done!"

Jacob shook his head and stood up from his shady seat. "Such a thing is indeed very wrong. But even the worst evils can fall out for good. Hear me, now. If this Shechem wishes to marry your sister—and I understand that *is* his wish—then we will take advantage of that desire!"

Joseph, who sat outside Dinah's tent, could not comprehend his father's view of things.

Caught away in possibilities, Jacob began to expound his vision.

"This will be our bride price," he asserted. "We will exact trade relations with the Hivites whereby our taxes will be lower. We will insist on a surtax on the goods we sell, so that they bring in extra revenue. Since we will be relatives, we will demand an unlimited lease on this property, so that Hamor can never evict us, or raise our rent.

"Furthermore," he enthused, his eyes sparkling, "when Dinah bears Shechem a son, ours will be a royal family, for the lad will be in line for the Hivite throne!"

Joseph was incredulous. So this was the side of his father which had made him notorious, which had exacted Esau's birthright for a bowl of porridge, which had taken the upper hand over Grandfather Laban's flocks by finding a way to make his own sheep and goats proliferate. Yes, this was the Jacob who had even deceived his own father, posing as Esau to win the patriarchal blessing!

To the boy's amazement, Jacob's reasoning appeared to please Reuben and Judah, who listened intently, their expressions eager.

But Joseph could see that Simeon and Levi were dissatisfied. Jacob did not seem concerned when the two of them leaned together, consulting privately. So confident was the patriarch in his own judgment that he assumed all the brothers saw the wisdom of his plan.

There would be no time for discussion, however. Across the Hivite plain, arising from the direction of Shalem, a great host approached. It appeared that every male of the city was in that throng, led by two men on white, prancing horses.

Joseph instantly recognized one as the Hivite prince, and his skin bristled.

Tall, dark, and grand, he rode ahead of the others, his chin held high, as though he had not within the last few hours committed a great crime.

To Jacob's youngest son he was a monster, and the lad clenched his fists. How he wished the elder brothers would take vengeance here and now! He would join them. He would fight beside them like a soldier.

Jacob saw things differently, however. All day long he had awaited this very moment. He had known Hamor and Shechem would not long delay in asking Dinah's hand.

But the clever elder would play his own hand craftily.

At the sound of the horde, the Jacobite tribe gathered on the rise, wondering what transpired. To this point, no one but Dinah, Jacob, and Jacob's sons knew the situation.

Among the uninformed tribespeople, the first thought was that the Hivites were on the attack. But when they saw that their leaders were unarmed, and that the advancing throng carried no weapons, they watched the drama in murmuring fascination.

Determined to appear nonchalant, Jacob returned to his seat and resumed twirling the foxtail reed in his fingers.

He did not see Dinah emerge from her mother's tent, fearful and wondering. But Joseph saw, and he noted the look of conflicted love she gave the dashing Shechem.

As soon as the girl appeared in the tent's distant shadow, Shechem likewise saw her. And the expression on his face could only be called adoration.

Joseph's stomach tensed. Protectiveness, anger, and jealousy struggled within him. But he had no right, being the youngest, to express them.

Hamor, reining his mount a courteous distance from Jacob, stepped down and bowed. Though this was his tenant and not his superior, he had come to ask something of him and must show respect.

The patriarch, knowing he had the upper hand, nodded to him coolly.

"Jacob, called Israel," Hamor began, "my people are neighbors with your people. I come as your friend."

The Hebrew, raising a skeptical eyebrow, made no reply.

Standing up, Hamor surveyed the angry faces of the eleven sons, their tense postures and clenched fists. "I shall not mince words," he said, clearing his throat. "I am sure you know why I have come."

Casting a wary glance at the brothers, he proceeded.

"The soul of my son, Shechem, longs for your daughter," he declared, bowing again. "I pray you, give her to him as his wife."

At this, Dinah blushed with joy, her eyes locking on Shechem's with girlish ardor.

But Hamor was not finished. "Furthermore," he suggested, "let us be allies in this wild land. Many are our enemies all about, who desire to take what we have. Let us make marriages among ourselves. Give us your daughters, and take our daughters for your sons.

"You shall dwell equally with us," he went on. "The land shall be yours to live in, conduct business in, and prosper in."

Jacob, stunned, sat white faced before the man. So far beyond his wild scheme was this offer that his incredulous ears tingled.

Judah and Reuben, likewise, scarcely concealed their astonishment. And when Shechem dismounted, falling reverently before the Hebrew, Jacob was mute with shock.

"Let me find grace in your eyes," the prince pleaded. "Whatever you shall ask of me, I shall give."

The young man's apparent sincerity was intensely appealing. Women in the tribe gasped, whispering together. And Dinah's cheeks were moist with tears.

"Ask anything at all, but please," he begged, "give me the maiden as my wife."

Jacob was speechless. At last, leaning down from his seat, he tapped the prostrate fellow on the shoulder and bade him arise.

Tenderly he studied the fervent countenance, and a smile stretched his lips.

But just as he would make reply, Simeon and Levi, who had been privately leaning together, hastened forward.

Crooked grins worked on their faces, and quickly they intercepted the dealings, as though they had the right.

"We cannot do this thing," Levi objected, trying to appear disappointed. "After all, you, being a Canaanite, are ... uncircumcised!"

Jacob shot a quizzical glance at the two intruders. But, again, before he could speak, Simeon interrupted.

"Yes, yes. It is against our tradition ... a reproach, actually, against our people."

"What?" Jacob tried to intervene. But Simeon talked over his head, and over the murmuring tribe.

"However," he suggested, rubbing his hands together, and playing at condescension, "we will consent if you will all be circumcised, every one of you. Then we will give you our young women, we will take your ladies for ourselves, and we will be your allies."

"Indeed," Levi added, seeing that Jacob stood angrily to his feet, "if you will *not* do this, we will take our sister and be gone!"

The patriarch, confounded, held his peace. He could not imagine why his sons insisted on imposing this bloody ordeal on the Canaanites. There was no regulation such as they described for the marriage of young Hebrew women. Yet to confront Simeon and Levi with their deception could only cast doubt on the integrity of his whole tribe. When Hamor looked at him suspiciously, Jacob only shrugged.

Dubious, the Hivites conferred among themselves. But when Hamor stepped again before Jacob, agreeing to the stipulation, the patriarch could do nothing but accept.

Shakily he called for Dinah.

The girl, seeing no one but her beloved, hastened from her mother's tent. In simple ceremony, Jacob placed her little hand in Shechem's, and the prince, mounting his horse, lifted her up behind him.

Dinah was thereby married, and Joseph watched her ride away, his eyes misting.

# 7

Three nights later, flames raged through the town of Shalem, leaping tall and orange against the black sky.

Whether it was the ominous glow of the pyre-like city or the frantic cries preceding it that roused Jacob's camp, within moments the entire tribe was alert.

Jacob scrambled out from Rachel's tent, his loincloth still loose upon his body, and Rachel peered out from her bed, grasping her blanket close to her chest.

Joseph, who did not share his mother's tent so often as he had when he was younger, had slept beneath the stars tonight. He, along with the shepherds of the hills, had been the first to hear the cries and see the fiery flashes lick the dark.

Flinging back the flap of his bedsack, he joined his father on the rise. Following close were the others: Reuben, Judah, Gad, Asher, Dan, Naphtali, Issachar, and Zebulun.

But where was Simeon, and where was Levi?

Quickly Jacob assayed the situation, and as the crafty plot of the missing sons dawned upon him, his face was a contortion of rage and shame.

"What have they done!" he cried, throwing his arms wide. Falling to the earth, he scraped up handfuls of dirt and poured them through his hair. "Jehovah!" he wept. "God Almighty, save us! What have they done!"

Reuben and Judah glanced at Joseph, who did not comprehend what evil had been perpetrated upon the Hivites. Drawing near the lad, Reuben bent close and whispered, "Simeon and Levi have dishonored our father. They have fallen on the Shechemites, who trusted us, and have taken them in their weakest hour."

Joseph's face clouded. He knew that "weakest hour" meant the time of debilitation which followed a man's circumcision.

Always the people of his tribe performed the rite when a baby was only eight days old. Something about that timing produced the least pain for the male. This they had learned through generations of experience. But the Shechemites had endured the surgery in the prime of life. The third day after circumcision was always the hardest.

Barely had Reuben spoken when their eyes were drawn to the gate of the city. Two figures emerged on horseback, followed by a contingency of Jacobites, all on foot. The onlookers recognized them instantly as Simeon, Levi, and their personal menservants, nearly fifty in all.

In their hands they brandished bloody swords and dripping scabbards, and upon their faces were gleaming grins. Shouting and laughing, they raced toward camp, Simeon carrying Dinah like a bag of barley, slung across the back of his saddle.

Flailing and kicking, the girl cried out for her beloved— for Shechem, who would never be hers or anyone else's again.

Joseph, too, cried out, matching her pain with his horror.

Racing down the hill, he was suddenly caught by Reuben's outstretched arm.

Frantically he looked into the man's kind face, and burying his head on his broad shoulder, he wept aloud.

"It is all my fault!" Joseph sobbed, imagining the city's helpless men, easy prey for the ruthless hunters and unable to defend their families. "It is my fault!"

"How is that, Little One?" Reuben queried.

"I should not have told Father about Shechem's crime," he replied, his chest heaving. "Dinah begged me not to. No one would have known ... no one would have died. ..."

"Enough," Reuben insisted, holding him close. "You were right to defend your sister's honor."

The lad's thoughts were a blur. As he saw Simeon and Levi draw near with their agonized sister, and as he observed his father, weeping and scraping upon the ground, he suddenly knew hatred as he had never known it.

Always Simeon and Levi had been his tormentors. Always they had been wild men. But never had he hated them.

Until now.

# 8

The fields of Hamor retreated in the night behind Jacob's fleeing caravan.

Joseph rode in the back of his mother's wagon, watching over the woman whose pale face reflected sadly in the moonlight.

Although the lad looked forward to the formal announcement of Rachel's pregnancy, he did worry over her health. Other women, he had observed, glowed like rubies when they were with child. But Rachel seemed frail, and rather than gaining the fleshly plumpness typical of others, she was thinner than ever.

Jacob was on the run again. For four years he had dwelt peaceably in the Jordan region, his struggle with Esau at an end and his hopes high for the future.

Now, under cover of dark he must once more play the part of the refugee. The Jacobites, or "Israelites" as they were becoming known, would not be welcome in Canaan once the many tribes and cities of the country learned of the havoc wreaked at Shalem.

It was autumn. Fields of charred stubble passed by, and Joseph could smell the ashes of the turned earth where farmers had burned their depleted plots in preparation for next year's crop. As the wheels of Rachel's wagon crunched over the rutted fields, Joseph knew his father avoided the main highway.

The only word Jacob had given his frightened tribe was that the Lord had told him to flee for Bethel, the place of his first encounter with the Almighty years before.

There he had first sought guidance after fleeing Esau's threats. There the angels of the Lord had appeared to him in a dream, coming and going upon a ladder stretched between earth and heaven.

And there, he hoped, his people would find sanctuary.

But more than tribal safety was at risk in this crisis. As Joseph observed his mother's wan countenance—the way her hands folded across her swollen belly, the way her despairing eyes wandered over the moonstruck fields—he wondered if this journey would require too much of her.

He knew that if it did, he would never forgive Simeon and Levi. He would never overlook their selfish need for power, and he would have even more reason to hate them.

# INTERLUDE

Joseph lay face down on the ridge of the Bethel-Ephrath mountains. The frigid earth with its unyielding frost was no comfort to the lad whose mother had just died in childbirth.

From somewhere overhead the haunting cry of a nighthawk, shrill and accusing, thrilled through the icy air.

Rachel was dead, and Joseph felt responsible.

Yes, his tormented heart insisted, if he had obeyed Dinah, if he had not betrayed her secret to his father, Simeon and Levi would not have invaded Shalem. The Israelites would still dwell at peace in Shechem Vale, and his mother would never have been forced to endure the harsh escape.

For a long while he lay prostrate, until the guilty thoughts were interrupted. At first he resisted the overriding refrain, the comfort which sprang from beyond himself, reminding him of the Hope of Israel, of the night his father had wrestled with the angel and had come out victor.

Sitting up, he put his hands to his ears as if to block the hope-filled impression.

*Joseph* had never seen an angel. *Joseph* had not been blessed with visions, as had his father.

And now that he was faced with the gravest loss of his young life, he disbelieved in them utterly.

As he sat fending off the persistent chords of promise, however, another voice invaded his solitude. Jacob had come to find him, putting his own fresh grief aside to quest after his heartbroken son.

Scrambling to his feet, Joseph stood numb and quivering in the blackness.

Surely he would die if his father found him. Surely any human touch would kill him.

Fleeing, he bounded across the ice-locked hills, slipping and sliding until his body lost contact with the earth.

Suddenly, unexplicably, Joseph was at the mouth of a cave. As his head whirled with a sense of the supernatural, he was stunned to see a fire within the rock room, and an ethereal figure silhouetted before it.

"Joseph, son of Jacob, behold," the figure addressed him.

Following the stranger's gesture, which directed him to gaze deep within the cave, Joseph stood up and rubbed his eyes.

Against the back wall, where the shadows and lights of the fire played, he perceived a scene drawn by some invisible finger—drawn for him alone. It seemed he and his brothers were binding sheaves in a field, and Joseph's sheaf, suddenly leaping to life, stood up. The other sheaves likewise arose, and turning to face Joseph's, bowed before it.

The lad, quaking, observed the image fade, and with it the mysterious stranger.

Bracing himself against the opening, he felt his knees buckle.

Whether the fire went out, or he only closed his eyes, Joseph knew not. But darkness, like a dream, caressed him.

\* \* \*

Strong hands lifted Joseph from the sun-streaked earth. Upon his body was the crisp dew of a winter morning, and where he had lain curled up at the cavern door, a thawed patch traced his outline.

Struggling for consciousness, he saw his father's face brooding above him.

As Joseph shook himself alert, he stared into the empty cave at the place where a fire had burned just hours before and a phantom figure had communed with him.

"Father," he stammered, "in there . . . a man . . ."

Jacob studied the hollow room, wondering what his son alluded to.

"A fire, Papa!" Joseph explained. "There was a fire in this very place."

But there was nothing in the cave save a few charred remains of some long-deserted camp.

"No one has been here for many years," Jacob insisted.

Suddenly struck by his father's grief-etched countenance, Joseph realized how much the bereft man needed him.

Together the two upheld each other as they ascended the ravine down which Joseph had skidded in the dark.

Only once did the boy look back, marking forever in his memory the place of his own Bethel.

# PART II
## The Dreamer

# 9

Jacob would not suffer his wife to be buried in the icy winter mountains. Instead, he led his people down the west side of the hills to the lovely hamlet of Bethlehem, and there he erected the pillar which would forever mark her grave.

Joseph stood, this morning, outside the village walls, watching as Jacob laid stone upon stone until the little monument was chest high.

Bilhah, Rachel's maid, also watched, the wriggling babe whom Rachel had named Ben Oni clutched to her breast. Tears streaked her face, but she was typically quiet, and Joseph wondered how she had felt living in Rachel's shadow.

All the women with whom Jacob was intimate—Leah, Zilpah, and Bilhah—had endured secondary status. Joseph had always taken it for granted that this was as it should be. His fair mother was the natural favorite.

But now, as he observed Bilhah apart from Rachel, it occurred to him that such a situation might not be a happy one for the lesser wives.

For an agonizing moment, his father studied the pillar. Then with a groan of resignation, he lifted the last stone into place.

Joseph saw Bilhah's chest heave, as though she had performed the task, and not her master.

In that instant the baby began to cry, and Jacob turned to the concubine, calling for the child.

Quickly the woman came forward, placing the tiny infant in his father's hands.

Turning his gaze heavenward, Jacob faced the pillar and raised the baby aloft.

"His name shall no more be Ben Oni, 'son of my sorrow,' " the patriarch announced. "Ben Jamin shall his name be, 'son of my right hand.' "

The infant, his feet kicking the sky, received his new calling without a whimper.

Though Benjamin would never know Rachel's touch or the sweet sound of her voice, he seemed content to be Jacob's child.

And though he could not know it now, young Joseph, who watched his christening with quiet pride, would love him as ardently as any mother.

\* \* \*

Joseph's heart was full that evening when he found his father meditating in the shade of a sycamore tree. Many emotions wrestled inside the lad—grief at the loss of his mother, joy at the gift of Benjamin, and wonder at the meaning of the encounter in the cave.

After a long day of setting up camp in Bethlehem's shepherd hills, a sense of urgency drove him to seek out Jacob. He had waited four years to ask about his father's struggle in the Gilead wilderness. He could wait no longer.

The boughs of the sycamore, beneath which Jacob sat, waved toward the fertile valley where Bethlehem nestled clean and white. A gentle breeze moved the branches in beckoning gestures.

Oblivious to Joseph's approach, the patriarch was caught away in private devotion. The lad, drawing near, lingered over the sight of his prayerful father, sure that he could never love Jacob more than he did at this moment.

Despite the trials of his life, Jacob was still a young man. His athletic body was lank and trim. His hair was black as night, and his beard was tinged with the same raging red that predominated in Esau's coloring. But as he sat with his face turned heavenward, afternoon sunlight spilled in patches through the leaves above, and Joseph noted fine streaks of silver at his temples.

Reverently the boy stepped forward, his shadow falling across Jacob's face. The elder jolted from his wistful meditation and smiled.

"Son," he said, "you startled me."

Joseph, fearing himself an intruder, stammered, "If you would rather be alone…"

"No, no," Jacob insisted. "I would have been coming home soon. Sit with me awhile."

The lad could see salty lines of dried tears upon his father's cheeks. He knew Jacob had been mourning Rachel, and the realization brought a tightness to his chest.

Joseph himself would be a long time grieving, although somehow the episode in the cave had helped ease his pain. But how he longed to discuss the mysterious encounter!

Leaning aside, Jacob bade Joseph sit with him, and as he did, the boy saw his father grimace from the pain of his bad hip.

"Papa," Joseph began, taking opportunity from what he observed, "I remember when your leg first began to trouble you."

This was said with much care. Jacob, unprepared for the topic, stared at Joseph in surprise.

"You do?" he marveled. "How is that possible? You were a mere baby!"

"I was six years old!" Joseph objected.

Jacob shook his head, chuckling. "Tell me, then… what do you remember?"

To Joseph the recollection was as clear as though it had happened yesterday, and not four years before.

"I remember that you disappeared into the wilderness on the day before you met Uncle Esau. And I remember that you were limping on that leg when you returned."

Jacob, seeing that his son's memory was correct, listened more seriously.

"I also remember that you took the name 'Israel' from that moment. And I know you fought with something ... or someone ... very powerful, as your new name implies."

For a long while the patriarch was silent, his thoughts far away.

"Papa, why have you never spoken of that night?" Joseph pressed him.

"Who would have believed me?" the man sighed. "Your mother, dear as she was, was confounded by too much of the supernatural. And your brothers ..." Jacob only shrugged.

The first admission was made tenderly. As for the second, Jacob did not need to explain. Joseph knew the elder brothers would have responded with bewilderment, if not outright scoffing.

"It *was* an angel then!" Joseph deduced, his eyes wide at the long-kept secret.

"It was," Jacob replied.

The patriarch's gaze traced the treetops as he relived the distant evening.

"I had been running from the Lord a very long time," he recounted. "My brother desired to kill me. But it was not Esau alone who pursued me. It was God Almighty."

His voice dropped as he confessed, "I did evil to Esau, and he had a right to avenge himself. The Lord was not pleased with me."

Gaining courage from the admission, the elder lifted his chin and carefully recounted the tale of how he had usurped Esau's birthright—how he had taken advantage of the man's ravenous hunger upon his return from an unsuccessful hunting expedition and had traded him a bowl of stew for his inheritance.

As he spoke, his eyes misted. Yet he told all: how he and his own mother, Rebekah, had plotted the deception of Father Isaac; how he had posed as Esau before the blind elder; and how he had fraudulently secured the patriarchal blessing—a blessing that could not be revoked.

"What I did was unpardonable," Jacob concluded, "but Esau has forgiven me."

Joseph, who had heard these talks from others, barely breathed. "But, Father, you wrestled with an angel!" he whispered.

Jacob knew the notion was intriguing. He knew his son must have exercised great self-restraint, keeping his curiosity in check all these years.

"I had lived so long with fear," Jacob softly explained, "that when the Lord appeared unto me, I could not let him . . . I *would* not let him go until he blessed me!"

"Yes?" Joseph marveled, urging his father on.

Jacob placed a hand on the lad's knee.

"You wish to know more," he surmised, a twinkle in his eye. "You want to know what he looked like, how strong he was, and how tall. You want to understand how a mortal man could fight with an angel of the Lord."

Joseph did not deny this, eagerly nodding his head.

Leaning back, the elder pulled his knees to his chest and thought such a great while that Joseph grew uneasy.

"How does one describe light brighter than light?" he began. "He came upon me like the wind, and he encompassed me on every side. He was a man, yet not a man. When he laid hands on me, and I on him, it was as though the universe spun about my head!"

Joseph thrilled to the conviction in his father's voice. "Did you struggle with him a long time?" he asked.

"All night, until dawn broke in the east," Jacob recalled.

"But surely . . ."

"I know what you are thinking," Jacob mused, patting him on the shoulder. "You consider that any angel of the Lord Almighty should have easily prevailed against me."

"Why . . . yes, sir," Joseph admitted, hoping he did not offend.

"Well," Jacob laughed, "that certainly occurred to me that night—and many times since. All I can conclude is that the Lord restricts himself from time to time, that he might reach into our lives."

"And he did that, Father!" Joseph enthused. "He gave you your blessing!"

Jacob clapped him on the back. "You are an able student, my child! You have a heart for things divine, and so you shall prosper."

Suddenly, with this encouragement, Joseph felt free to speak of the cave. He was about to declare the vision he had received, to revel openly in the notion that one day he would be blessed, that one day he would prevail over his brothers. But Jacob was not finished. As he gave his conclusion, Joseph was chagrined.

"Truly," he said, "the Lord did bless me. The memory alone of that encounter is precious, but the outcome more valuable than gold. He gave me a new name and a second chance," he testified. "But most precious of all, he restored love between me and my brother."

The patriarch paused, his throat tight with feeling. And Joseph listened, red faced.

"If you learn nothing else in this life," Jacob asserted, "learn this: brotherhood is a gift of God, and loss of goodwill between friends is a dagger to the soul. But God is a friend who sticks closer than a brother."

"Brotherhood . . ." Joseph recoiled at the term. Images of Simeon and Levi returning from the destruction of Shalem burned within him. He would far rather they bowed before him, like the sheaves on the cave wall, than that they be his friends. He would far rather that Gad and Asher and all the others groveled at his feet.

As his father continued to expound his philosophy, Joseph had leaden ears.

"The reward did not come easily," Jacob asserted. "The angel of God did not restore my brother to me without exacting a price. Every time I limp upon my sorry leg, I am reminded of my dependence on the Lord."

The son was silent, wishing now that he had not pursued this discussion.

Jacob, seeing his downcast expression, sensed the contents of his heart, the lifetime of hurt which had shriveled his soul. Drawing the lad to his bosom, he went on, "I asked the angel his name that night. He refused to tell me. But I myself gave a name to the place of my struggle."

Joseph avoided his father's somber gaze.

" 'Peniel,' I called it," Jacob said, " 'the face of God.' For I had seen the Lord face to face, and my life was preserved."

Sunset was coming upon them, and a cool breeze filled the mountainside with the smell of early spring. Joseph, resisting his father's embrace, leaned rigidly against him, listening to the rhythm of his heart.

"If you seek God's face," the elder exhorted, "he is able to make all men to be at peace with you. Remember this, my son, and you will do well."

# 10

The Oaks of Mamre! Joseph had heard of them all his life. Today, the last day of his twelfth year, he was privileged to see them.

From high atop his father's finest camel, he spied their lush greenery miles before the caravan reached the destination. Billowy, almost black against Canaan's yellow grass and rolling hills, they rose. He thrilled to the sight.

For it was here that Grandfather Abraham had settled, nearly two centuries ago, after entering this land.

Tomorrow would be Joseph's thirteenth birthday, the day of his initiation into Hebrew manhood. A full week ago, Jacob had announced that his tribe must move south, for he would have Rachel's firstborn meet Grandfather Isaac on the day he became a man.

Little Benjamin, who was nearly three years old, rode with Joseph, propped between his legs on the camel's swaying saddle.

"See there!" Joseph directed, pointing to the forested hills. "That is where our Grandpa lives. He is a very old man, and very wise."

Benjamin, whose luminous lavender eyes followed Joseph's finger, sat up straight. "Will he know me?" he asked.

"Papa has told him about you," Joseph replied. "Papa's messengers are always carrying word of Benjamin."

Pleased with that answer, the little boy settled back against Joseph's chest, and the older brother studied his raven curls, so like Rachel's.

As the caravan wound down the fertile slopes toward Mamre, a shout of greeting met them from across the valley. To everyone's amazement, another train could be seen approaching the Oaks from the east, and no one could have mistaken the leader of the vast host.

It was Esau who cried the greeting—Esau upon his black mount—Esau with his crimson beard.

Jacob, who walked alongside Leah's wagon, took off at a full run. Leaping across gullies and hills he tore jubilantly toward his elder brother.

Esau likewise jumped to the ground and ran to join him.

Racing across the valley, they met before Isaac's tent. There would surely be a party in Mamre tonight!

\* \* \*

Grandfather Isaac had dwelt so long at Mamre, that he was no longer a nomad. In fact, he had some years ago built a riverstone meetinghouse on the property where his great tribe held councils and worshiped Jehovah.

When Joseph first laid eyes on him, it was in that meetinghouse.

All evening the three tribes—Jacob's, Esau's and Isaac's—partied outside together, hundreds of merrymakers celebrating the family reunion and anticipating Joseph's bar mitzvah. Music and wine flowed freely, girls danced and men sang, until the forest's living rafters trembled.

And all evening, Joseph shot glances toward the council hall, wondering when he would see his grandfather, the elder, who had not emerged.

Isaac was seated at the council fire when Joseph, Jacob and Esau at last entered the building. It was midnight, and breaking into the first day of Joseph's thirteenth year. The lad's eleven brothers and Esau's sons joined them, waiting along the back wall as Joseph was ushered forth for formal introduction to the patriarch.

Through the dim and smoky interior he was led, past rows of smiling faces. Men all about reached out to greet his father and uncle, men who had known Jacob and Esau from birth and who now waited to receive Joseph into their fraternity.

Enthusiastically they hailed the youngster. At first he could hardly conceive that these people honored him. But ahead sat his grandfather, and when he saw him, the warmth of acceptance flooded over him.

In the orange fireglow, the old man was beautiful, his noble face translucent but smooth as a youth's. His patriarchal beard reached nearly to his lap, shining with silver and with the sheen of affectionate grooming. Though his filmy eyes were nearly sightless, he could make out his two sons and the beloved boy in the firelight, and his expression seemed to say he had awaited this moment for a lifetime.

To Rachel's firstborn, the firstborn of Jacob's heart, this was a hallowed hour. As long as he could remember, he had dreamed of meeting Isaac. He trembled as he came before him, as though he entered the sanctuary of God Almighty.

Indeed, Isaac was a living chronicle, the closest man to Abraham, Shem, Noah, or Adam, who walked the earth.

As Jacob and Esau reached down to embrace their father, the old man quaked terribly. The last time he had seen either son, the two had been at war. Jacob had stolen Esau's birthright, had deceived his father, and had fled. Esau, bent on killing him, had pursued him nearly to Padan-Aram.

Now the entire nation was reunited, the feud no longer separating tribe from tribe.

As Jacob and Esau sat down on either side of the patriarch, Isaac reached out his arms to receive Joseph. Falling into his grandfather's embrace, the lad felt the old man's tears upon his neck.

"Bone of my bone, flesh of my flesh!" Isaac cried. "How my soul has yearned for you!"

Releasing him, he held him at arm's length.

"My eyesight is very dim," he admitted, "but my hands see for me."

With this, he traced Joseph's youthful face with his fingertips, reading it like a scroll.

"Your features are beautiful, as Rachel's must have been. And your shoulders," he exclaimed, grasping him firmly, "they are broad as Jacob's!" Then leaning back, he proclaimed, "So they should be! For today you are a man!"

As if on cue, a small group of musicians, seated in a corner, began to play—timbrels thumping, lutes strumming, and pipes whistling.

Isaac clapped his hands, and as he did so, the crowd began to sing:

"O Lord, our Lord, how excellent is your name in all the earth! You have set your glory above the heavens. Out of the mouths of young ones you have ordained strength."

Emerging from other smoky corners, young girls came forth, strewing garlands up the aisle, dancing and twirling about Joseph.

As the music at last subsided, Isaac called for a cup of wine.

"This is the hour of your manhood," he announced. Joseph humbly took the cup and drank it.

Again, as soon as he was done, music began and the scene was repeated.

This time, as Joseph was traded from hand to hand among the dancing maidens, he was a little lightheaded. But now his father stood, and the crowd grew quiet once more.

"A man should look the part of a man!" Jacob cried, commanding everyone's attention. "A prince should look the part of a prince! Therefore," he said, reaching into a fold of his long cloak, "I present you with your royal coat!"

Suddenly unfurled before the audience was a magnificent garment—a long, striped tunic of many colors.

Joseph, dazzled, stepped forward and caressed the fabric. He recognized it immediately as his mother's handiwork, a project she must have spent years secretly pursuing.

Between each stripe, separately woven, was intricate stitchery of gold and silver. And upon each stripe, broad as a man's hand, were emblems of the nomad life: tiny sheep and goats, camels and tents and shepherd staffs.

Never had there been such a coat—a bar mitzvah coat befitting a tribal prince!

"Turn around," Jacob said proudly.

Before the onlookers, the father draped the tunic over Joseph's back. And the crowd applauded.

Little Benjamin, who had been watching from the rear of the room, from the height of Reuben's shoulders, squirmed to join his brother. Lowered to the floor, he ran forward, leaping proudly into Joseph's arms.

But the ceremony was not complete.

Isaac had yet to give the patriarchal blessing. Silence filled the long chamber as Isaac lifted his arms.

"Son of Jacob, son of Israel," he began, "the least shall become greatest, the last shall be first!" His words ringing with prophetic conviction, he declared: "Joseph, you shall be a savior to your people, the rescuer of your brothers and their strong deliverer. Have faith in God. You shall rise above all your enemies, and having the power of life and death, shall turn to save them."

An awesome hush thrilled through the congregation, and Jacob's ten elder sons stared mutely at their younger brother.

Was Joseph not merely the son of a second wife? Was he not inferior to the sons of Leah, and younger than the sons of Bilhah and Zilpah?

Levi and Simeon cast sideways smirks at each other, while Reuben and Judah murmured uneasily.

But now the musicians played again, indicating it was time to exit the council chamber.

Joseph, heady with the prophecy, the night, and the wine, carried his chin high, and Benjamin, riding in his arms, nestled proudly against him.

The honored Bar Mitzvah, Son of Israel, passed by his elder brothers in his princely robe, heedless of their anger.

He knew they resented him. But then, they always had.

# 11

Stars, like fiery prisms, studded the black sky. Joseph lay upon his back, his arms folded under his head as he studied the depths of the ebony night.

His priceless tunic was his pillow, carefully rolled and held beneath his neck as though he would defend it with his life.

Over and over he relived the evening. Isaac's ageless face dominated his reverie, and his amazing words resounded through Joseph's mind.

"You shall be a savior to your people . . . a savior . . . a savior . . ."

Contemplating possible interpretations, Joseph was filled with wonder. Just how could the tribe of Israel ever be so needy? And how could he alone save them?

He was too young and too unwise to be humbled by the prophecy. Throughout his entire life he had bowed to the shadows of his ten elder brothers. Isaac's words filled him with more eager pride than was becoming.

He sensed that the prediction paralleled his experience in the cave. Closing his eyes, he reconstructed the scene on the cave wall: the sheaves of his brothers bowing to his sheaf.

Of course they would bow! he reasoned. If he were to someday be their savior, they would surely make obeisance!

Opening his eyes again, he was captivated by an eerie movement in the summer sky. Whereas before, the stars, the moon, and the planets were in their natural positions, they were now strangely altered. Several stars, eleven to be exact, had formed a row in front of a twelfth, which seemed much brighter than they.

The moon also joined the lesser stars, and as Joseph watched, the sky was filled with light like the light of day. For the sun appeared as well, standing beside the moon.

Joseph blinked and shielded his eyes from the glare.

Despite the fact that the sun had appeared, the stars were still clearly visible. And to his amazement, the twelfth star shone as brightly as ever.

As the celestial bodies held these new positions, Joseph sensed that the eleven lesser stars, the sun, and the moon were honoring the twelfth and solitary star.

His skin was gooseflesh. Shaking himself, he sat up, trying to clear his head. But the peculiar phenomenon— the night turned to day, the day within the dark—did not depart.

It was not until Joseph was distracted from the amazing witness by a disturbance in camp that the sky returned to normal.

A sound of weeping and mourning had arisen from the vicinity of Isaac's tent.

Joining the other people who emerged from their shelters and their beds to investigate the matter, Joseph went hastily to the common.

In the still of the night, Isaac had passed away. The venerable elder, the one who had known Abraham, had been gathered to his fathers, 180 years old and full of joy at the reunion of his children.

As Joseph heard this, he suddenly cared little for the stars. He would have preferred more time in Isaac's presence to a thousand inscrutable visions.

# 12

The autumn fields beyond the Oaks of Mamre were wet with dew. Pink sunlight traced a halo across the valley, just breaking through the clinging mist that cloaked the verdant earth.

Seventeen-year-old Joseph hoisted his knapsack higher on his back and breathed deeply of the moist air. So fine a morning he had not seen in a long time.

The dew quickly seeped through his sandals and absorbed into the thick stockings that bound his feet. But he did not mind. He was off to find Dan and Naphtali, Gad and Asher, the sons of his father's concubines.

All summer he had served as a groom in the tribal corral, caring for the white and speckled horses which were Jacob's special pride. Shepherding suited him much better. To be out in the fields, beneath the stars, was to Joseph the closest thing to heaven. And to share in his brothers' manly conversation, the closest thing to complete fulfillment he had ever known.

Of all his brothers, he was most comfortable with the sons of Bilhah and Zilpah. True, there were times of tension between them. He noted this especially when he wore the parti-colored cloak that Jacob had presented at his bar mitzvah.

He would be sure to take it off and conceal it in his pack before he reached the shepherd camp. But for now, as he passed along the stream that watered the Oaks, he wore the garment proudly.

Perhaps it was inexperience, perhaps it was his pre-occupation with the glorious morning, but Joseph was oblivious to the admiring whispers of the maidens who knelt beside the stream doing the day's laundry. He was no longer the slight boy who had entered manhood in Isaac's council hall. He was no longer the awkward youngster who had danced with the girls the night of his bar mitzvah. But neither was he very moved by the beguiling glances that followed him when he walked through camp.

Taking after Great-grandfather Abraham, Grandfather Isaac and Father Jacob, the lad was striking in appearance. Tall as a young poplar, he stood out easily in a crowd, and he hoped that someday he might match Reuben for stature or Simeon for strength.

But most of all, he cradled in his satchel of dreams the mystery of the visions he had seen. And he wondered how they would be fulfilled.

Running his hand down the front of his princely coat, he smiled to himself as he reached the borders of Mamre, and trekked toward the pastures of fellowship. Passing coolly beyond the gazes of the maidens, he went in quest of the shepherds.

It was a fine thing to be a man, life stretching before him as fertile as the Hebron Valley.

\* \* \*

The high shepherd fields where Joseph's brothers would be found were a half-day's journey from Mamre. It was nearly sunset when he located the glowing campfire marking their site.

Though a nippy fall wind spilled over the hills, he removed his striped tunic and donned a simpler one, rolling his fine garment into a ball and concealing it in his knapsack.

As he came upon the four brothers and their servants, gathered for the evening about a simmering stewpot, the sound of lively music warmed him. Someone played a small harp and someone else accompanied him on a flute.

"Joseph!" Asher cried, slurring the word over his wine-soaked tongue. "Join us! Join us! What brings you here?"

The youngster entered the circle of flickering light, and Gad, slapping him on the back and giving a besotted smile, made room for him upon the felled log that served as a seat.

"Father sent me," Joseph replied. Merrily he took the crescent-shaped wineskin that was thrust into his hands.

"Father...good old Father!" Naphtali laughed, hoisting another skin and declaring a toast. "To Father!"

A round of inarticulate cheers followed this, and fellows all about the circle directed the spouts of their bottles toward their open mouths, catching the maroon liquid on their tongues.

"To Father, and to Great-grandfather Abraham!" Dan added.

Again the skins were turned bottoms up, and the gang laughingly imbibed.

"To Father, and to Great-grandfather Abraham, and don't forget Grandfather Isaac!" Asher bellowed.

Hilarity ensued, and Joseph found himself swept up in the mood.

This was what he had come out for—not for the shepherding alone, but for the companionship.

Gad, who seemed most affected by the evening's frivolity, sat uncomfortably close to Joseph. His vinegar breath was hot against the youngster's neck, and he seemed to study him too closely with his bloodshot eyes.

Joseph pulled away and focused on the others, until Gad's merry spirit turned sullen.

"Yes," Gad slobbered, "dear old Isaac. Of course, he never welcomed the rest of us into his fraternity as he welcomed you, Joseph. But he was a good man. He never gave us a bar mitzvah like the one he gave you. But he was a good man."

Joseph cringed as Gad leered in his face. He did not like the man's tone. All too quickly the boundary had been crossed between wine-warmed fondness and surly belligerence.

As others about the fire began to pick up on Gad's resentment, Joseph grew even more uneasy.

"Of course," Asher joined in, "Father Jacob never gave any of us a royal coat like the coat he gave our little brother. But he's a good man, too."

"Yes, yes," shouted Dan and Naphtali, and the servants howled with them.

"But, Little One is not wearing his coat tonight!" Dan noted. "Maybe it's not good enough for him any longer."

Suddenly, Naphtali leaned forward, snatching Joseph's satchel and rummaging through it.

"Aha!" he cried, pulling out the striped coat and waving it in the air. "I knew he wouldn't go anywhere without this!"

Instantly, the rowdy group turned on the youngster, slinging irrational accusations.

"So, we weren't fit company for your royal robe!" Asher spat. "You'd wear it for the sheep, but not for us!"

"No, you don't understand . . ." Joseph tried to defend himself.

But his brothers' hostility only escalated.

He would never be able to recount the next few moments. In a blur of movement and thrashing, he was tackled from the log and thrown to the ground. All about him were scuffling feet and pounding fists.

Somehow he managed to regain himself, and stood shaking in their midst as they gritted their teeth and hurled epithets at him.

Fists clenched, he rallied and began flailing, revealing to his brothers the prophecies which he had so long harbored.

"You will all be sorry!" he shouted, his feet kicking and his fists flying. "Someday all of you will cry out to me for mercy! Then see how I shall avenge myself!"

Asher was on top of Joseph, his meaty hand forcing Joseph's head against the earth. "What's that, Little One?" he laughed. "Have you been dreaming?"

Gad, whose besotted brain managed amazed curiosity, tried to intervene.

"Come, Asher! Off of him! Let us hear what this dreamer has to say!"

With that, Asher drew back, but still sat on top of Joseph and would not let him go.

"So, we shall beg for mercy?" he scowled. "You, young mongrel, son of a second wife, should be pleading right now for your life!"

Again, Gad tugged on Asher, and the other two brothers assisted him.

"Let him speak!" they implored. "This should be good for a laugh."

At last, Asher stood up, glaring down on the lad who lay sprawled in the dust. Joseph, climbing out from between Asher's legs, brazenly pointed a finger in his face.

"Indeed, I have dreams. The same dreams that Isaac must have had when he foretold that I would one day have the power of life and death over you!"

Murmuring together, the crowd was pricked by the memory. Still enraged, they snarled at him to expound his point.

"Twice have I seen visions!" Joseph declared. "Twice has Jehovah shown me that you will one day bow to me!"

As they glared hatefully at him, he related the dreams of the sheaves and the stars. And the men, despising him as never before, kept their distance, silent as stilled lions.

A breeze off Hebron rose over the hill, cold and frightening. The flames of the dying fire jerked like spasmodic fingers.

It was Asher who broke the ominous pall, his voice as low as a stalking bear's.

"Will you indeed reign over us! Will you indeed have dominion over us!" With this, he threw a piercing kick to Joseph's side.

Naphtali, more troubled by the prophecy than he cared to admit, grasped Asher about the waist and held him tight.

Joseph, scrambling to his feet, scurried toward his satchel, stuffed his offcast coat into the bag and headed for the dark whence he had come.

"I shall tell Father how you have treated me!" he warned, disappearing into the night.

The brothers, nervously eyeing one another, began to laugh again and swagger about the fire, pretending masculine indifference. But their careless mood would not be easily recaptured.

# 13

Dinah knelt before Joseph, washing and dressing the scrapes upon his shins and arms in the low light of Jacob's tent. Fussing over him like a mother, the girl who had never married again after losing Prince Shechem was in her element.

"How could you let them do this to you?" she complained. "You know better than to make your elder brothers angry."

Joseph, who had tolerated her fretful nursing, pulled away. "You speak to me as though I were a child!" he growled.

"And so perhaps you are," Jacob countered, pacing the tent floor in frustration. "Can't I send you out to the fields without worrying for your safety?"

Young Benjamin, who sat in a corner holding Joseph's striped coat upon his lap, observed the interchange in tense silence. He knew what it was to be one of the lesser brothers, what it was to be rejected by the elder ten. And he understood how easily Joseph must have fallen prey to their vindictiveness.

But he said nothing, sensing that Father Jacob was in no mood for explanations.

"They were drunk," Joseph protested. "They were spoiling for a fight!"

"You needn't have given them one," Jacob argued. "What did you do to inflame them, anyway?"

At this, Joseph looked away, wishing to avoid the issue. But his father grew more persistent.

"They made fun of my coat and scorned the blessing Isaac bestowed on me," Joseph revealed.

Jacob stopped his pacing and placed a hand on Joseph's knee. His eyes evinced sympathy, and he would have let the matter go, had Leah not appeared in the doorway.

Entering her husband's tent with an armload of clean laundry, she deposited it on Jacob's bed. When she saw that Joseph had returned, she scrutinized his sorry condition in the lamplight.

"What happened to you?" she snapped, her hands on her hips.

With Rachel's death, Leah had attained full matriarchal position in the tribe. By the law of the nomad, she had always been the "first wife," but so long as her sister had lived, that status had been a legal one only. Though Jacob would never love her as he had loved Rachel, she now had no competitor, and wielded her rights like a sword.

"It is nothing, Mother," Jacob intervened, calling her by the term that made Joseph's skin bristle. "The boy ran into some trouble in the hills. He will be fine."

Of course, he avoided reference to the elder brothers. Though they were the sons of his concubines, he knew Leah would eagerly take their side against Joseph.

Leah hastily surveyed the youngster's scrapes and bruises, and shrugged indifferently.

"Best keep him at home," she said. "He is apparently not ready for men's work."

Joseph looked at the floor, and Benjamin started angrily, but the elder brother silenced him with a glance.

When the woman had left the tent, Jacob wiped his hands nervously on his cloak. "Dinah, Benjamin, leave us now," he commanded. "I would be alone with your brother."

Hesitant, the girl rose, taking her bowl of water and the rag with which she had cleansed Joseph's wounds. Benjamin, tenderly placing the royal coat about Joseph's shoulders, followed his sister into the yard, and Jacob pulled the tent flap closed behind them.

Carefully studying his son again, he knelt before him, gazing into his pensive face.

"We cannot have dissension in our tribe," the father said.

"I know," Joseph agreed, feeling quite hopeless.

"Have you told me everything?" Jacob probed. "I must know everything that happened."

Taking a deep breath, Joseph braced himself. "There is more," he confessed. "But . . . they pushed me to it!"

When Jacob only eyed him insistently, he shook his head in dejection.

"I told them a prophecy, Father. Something I had never told a soul . . . not even you."

"A prophecy?" Jacob marveled.

"Do you remember how you found me in the hills after Rachel's death? How you found me at the mouth of a cave, and how I told you I had seen a man inside that cave?"

"I do," Jacob recalled. "You had been dreaming."

"Perhaps," Joseph said. "But what is a dream? I have had other impressions since, whether awake or asleep. And I never told a soul until I told my brothers."

With this he unveiled the secrets of his heart, the visions so long withheld from his father.

As he described the images on the cave wall, the sheaves that obviously represented his brethren, and their act of obeisance, Jacob listened patiently.

When he related the vision of the eleven stars, however, the man grew tense.

"The sun and the moon, as well, bowed down before me," Joseph concluded, barely speaking above a whisper.

At this, Jacob lurched away, standing to his feet and pounding his fists into his thighs.

"So this is what you told them! What sort of dream is

this? Will I and your mother and your brothers indeed bow ourselves to the ground before you?"

Angrily the patriarch resumed his pacing, a scowl of wounded pride etched deep into his face.

Joseph had hesitated to mention the sun and the moon. The fact that Jacob interpreted them to represent Leah and himself came as no surprise.

The youngster had no idea how to assuage the hurt this inflicted. And as Jacob castigated him, tears flowed down Joseph's cheeks.

"You are lucky they did not kill you!" the elder cried. "Wars have been sparked by less than this."

Indeed, in their culture dreams and prophecies were not taken lightly. Whether or not folks agreed with the dreamer was of little consequence. Dreams exposed the heart, and the products of Joseph's heart bespoke a haughty spirit.

"Father...I..." he stammered.

People were gathering outside Jacob's tent, guessing at the reason for the shouting. And Jacob hushed his son.

"I cannot help what I dream," the lad objected, his voice low and cautious. "What would you have me do? Cut off my head?"

Anxious, he twisted the edge of his coat in his sweaty hands. "You have never told anyone but me about your fight with the angel," he asserted. "You knew you could trust me to honor you. Why, don't you honor *my* visions, *my* struggle?"

Jacob stared in amazement at his daring son. For a long while he said nothing, but when he did at last open his mouth, it was in command.

"You were to serve in the fields," he declared. "I shall not let you shirk your duty. Gad, Asher, Dan, and Naphtali were due to leave for Shechem today, where your other brothers are pasturing their flocks. If you had not stirred up this trouble, you would have been on your way with them. Come," he ordered. "I will send you to them."

"Yes, sir," Joseph obeyed, following Jacob into the yard.

Shame filled the lad. Never had he questioned his father. If Jacob said he was to blame, perhaps he was.

The people outside the tent moved out of the way and the elder called for a satchel of fresh food and a skin of wine. Placing the satchel on Joseph's back, he tightened the straps and then slapped the boy on the shoulder.

"Go now," he insisted, his voice cracking. "See if it is well with your brothers and with the flock, and bring me word again."

Sunset was settling over the camp. Joseph must find his way through the wilderness in the dark. And he must not look back.

As Jacob watched him depart, a chill passed through the patriarch. Remembering Isaac's words, that one day Joseph would save them all, that one day they would prostrate themselves before the lad, the elder trembled.

His stomach tight as a knot, Jacob passed back through the bewildered crowd and sought the sanctuary of his tent.

But he would not shake the message of Joseph's dreams any more easily than he had shaken the angel's grip upon his thigh.

# 14

Cold sunlight, traveling with the wind down the slopes of Shechem and warning of winter, smarted Joseph's eyes.

Five days ago he had left Mamre, his limbs still stinging from his fight in the Hebron hills. The past two days he had wandered through the high fields to which Jacob had commissioned him, seeking his brothers, intruding upon the camps of strangers, and inquiring vainly after the sons of Jacob.

As always, the hills of Shechem were choice grazing ground, better than any Jacob had found since he and his tribe had dwelt here.

Seven years had passed since Simeon and Levi had devastated the city of Shalem, surely long enough for the memory to fade and for Israelites to traffic safely among the itinerants of the region. Among the dozens of tribes who wandered annually through the area, the men of Mamre should not draw special censure.

Still, no one seemed to have seen them or heard of their whereabouts among the many shepherd camps where Joseph inquired.

On this, his fifth day of travel, Joseph numbly woke to daylight's call and drew his cloak tight. Beneath the heavy outer garment was his striped coat. He was determined to wear it this time. He would bear the mark of his calling when he came upon his kin. And he would be as warm as possible in the meanwhile.

As of last night, when chilling dark had descended, he still had not despaired of finding the elder ten. But the hope that should have been nurtured by the wakening day was shriveling.

His stiff joints resisted the sun's freezing fingers. Another hour of bleak questing would surely defeat him.

Painfully he rose to his knees, rolling his bed into a ball and stuffing it into his bag.

Scraping crystallized dew from bent fronds of field grass, Joseph let it melt in his hand and swiped it across his face. He did not know which way to go. He had searched all of the common sanctuaries of the shepherds. He wondered, now, if his brothers had ever been here.

Trying to feel determined, he struck out once again across the fields until he came to a westward swale. Down to the left lay the Vale of Shalem. Black ruins still marked the site where Prince Shechem's lovely city once stood.

Viewing the evidence of his brothers' wickedness, his imagination suddenly ran wild.

Suppose, he thought, suppose someone, coming on his brothers' camp, had recognized them. Suppose their dress or their speech had betrayed them as Israelites to one who was an enemy.

Joseph's preoccupation with his own troubles was pushed aside as thoughts of his brothers' welfare consumed him. Running through the fields, heart drumming, he cried out, "Reuben! Judah! Simeon!"

Anxiously he scanned the hills, fearing that any moment he would lay eyes on a bloodsoaked field, fearing he would find torn bodies and ransacked tents.

At night it had been easy to mark the sites of the various shepherd camps, for each had its own campfire showing its position in the hills. But during the day, when the shepherds followed their flocks, there was no telling where they might be found, no telling which bend in the path might bring Joseph upon an enemy's fold.

As he rounded a low bluff, against which puffs of dark heather were pressed by the wind, he was greeted by the aroma of roasting meat.

Assuming that he was approaching another group of strangers, and that they would not welcome his intrusion at breakfast time, he climbed the bluff, and lying on his stomach, tentatively peered over the edge.

Indeed he had come upon a camp. But it was a very small one, occupied by only one man.

Sitting beside his little fire, the shepherd huddled beneath a hooded cloak and held a long stick over the flames, upon which was skewered a succulent piece of partridge.

Joseph's mouth watered as he watched the morsel sizzle above the fire.

Though the shepherd's face was concealed by his hood, a whispy white beard, reaching nearly to his lap, showed that he was an elderly fellow. His hand, also, turning the stick, was veined and wizened, and Joseph wondered what he was doing all alone in this wild country.

Mostly, however, Joseph contemplated the food, knowing for the first time how Esau must have felt when he came upon Jacob and his fragrant stew after days without a decent meal. "Almost would *I* sell *my* birthright for a taste of that partridge!" he thought, recalling Esau's foolish bargain.

Lying close to the earth, the young man gazed longingly upon the browning meat.

"Why don't you join me?" the old man called.

Joseph's heart leaped. He had made no sound, having learned at an early age how to be quiet in the hills. Nor had the old fellow so much as lifted his eyes to the bluff. How he had discerned Joseph's presence, the young spy could not imagine.

Still, the shepherd seemed friendly enough. Scrambling down from the hiding place, Joseph accepted his offer and within seconds was rubbing his cold hands over the welcoming fire.

Ravenous, he devoured the roasted partridge which was generously portioned out to him, and it was not until he was satisfied that he took a keener interest in his host.

When he did, it was with some uneasiness for the old man studied him with a penetrating gaze.

"What are you looking for out in these hills?" the fellow asked.

It was a reasonable question, but something in the way it was put implied the stranger already knew the answer.

Joseph could not tell by the man's accent what tribe or what country he was of. Nor did his woolen mantle bear any distinctive design or emblem. In fact, if anything distinguished the man, it was the directness of his manner and the stark simplicity of his garb.

"I . . . I seek my brothers," Joseph answered. "Can you tell me where they are grazing their flocks?"

Somehow he sensed this was all he need reply. Somehow he felt the elder needed no further detail.

"They have moved on from here," the man replied. "I heard them say, 'Let's go to Dothan.' "

The fact that the shepherd seemed to know exactly who Joseph's brothers were, and where they were headed, did not strike the youngster as strange. Perhaps later it would seem peculiar, but for now, as he sat in his presence, warm and secure, it was perfectly plausible.

"Dothan?" Joseph marveled. "They told no one they were heading further north. They must have been afraid to stay in Shechem."

Joseph spoke to himself, but he felt that the old man knew exactly what he meant.

"I must find them," he insisted, standing up from the fire.

Bowing low, he thanked the man for his kindness and picked up his knapsack to be going.

Something in the old fellow's expression, however, gave him pause. Sadness, longing . . . feelings which mystified the youngster.

"I will be all right," Joseph heard himself saying.

The shepherd nodded, a knowing gleam in his eye. "Jehovah is with you," he said.

With this, Joseph smiled and turned to go. As he walked into the morning wilderness, he glanced back once to wave goodbye.

But the old man was gone, and the place where the fire had burned was merely a cold circle, charred upon the winter ground.

# 15

Reuben sat upon the edge of a great cistern, a heavy saddle slung across his lap. His hands, slathered with mutton grease, hastily worked the surface of the saddle, forcing the tallow into the leather.

But his mind was not on his work.

Nervously he watched the highway which passed nearby. He and his brothers had come upon the oasis early in the day. If no one challenged their right to the site by nightfall, they would be able to camp here and pasture their flocks in the choice fields that ran along the road for a month or even more.

Such a location was enviable. Because caravans traveling from Syria to Egypt made this their regular route, shepherds fortunate enough to dwell here could live comfortably for extended periods of time, buying their needed food and supplies from the merchants who passed by.

To be in such a situation in the wintertime was highly desirable. Abiding in the hills at this time of year was especially dangerous, with prowling beasts finding prey hard to come by. Not only were shepherds' flocks in greater peril, but all too often had men themselves lost their lives to ice-bound wolves and lions.

Of course, part of what had convinced the brothers to move north from Shechem was fear of the local tribes. They had encountered no trouble during their brief stay near Shalem Vale, but Dothan was a safer place.

Beside the cistern where Reuben sat was another well of the same size, its steep sides sloping a full ten feet toward a dry bottom. In the spring, torrents of rain and groundwater would nearly fill the little reservoirs, making this oasis a stopping place for every caravan going by. For now, however, it would be possible for a family such as Reuben's to abide here unhindered.

Still, until night fell, by the law of the nomad, the Jacobites' right to stay here could be challenged. If the challenger had a larger flock and more men in company, he would win the site.

The likelihood of such a thing happening was remote. The ten brothers and all their helpers were a formidable group. But Reuben would not rest until the sun fell toward the great sea hidden in the west.

Beyond the cisterns, his brothers were already setting up the huge camp that would serve them for several weeks. Reuben's horse, tethered to the well, nudged him with its speckled nose.

"Supper will be soon," the master laughed. Pointing to the orange sun, which was veiled by a winter fog, he reckoned the time. "Supper for the two of us, in one hour."

As twilight descended, so did a cold wind off the range to the east. Apparently no strangers would be challenging Reuben's men tonight. Given the nature of the season, any shepherd clans in the region would have already begun bedding down their flocks for the night.

Reuben was pleased with himself for having decided to move on to Dothan. Only one thing disturbed his peace of mind as he gathered up his heavy saddle and his grease pot and prepared to join his brothers in the field beyond.

When the sons of Bilhah and Zilpah had joined with the others in Shechem, they had boasted of their encounter with Joseph. Scoffing about the lad's prophecies, they revealed how they had repaid the braggart, and they were applauded by all but himself and Judah, who kept very quiet.

Reuben may have been hesitant to show it at times, but he loved Joseph dearly and was glad that at least the youngster was now safe at home with Jacob and Benjamin. Anger boiled in him at the callousness and unending hatred which his brethren had always manifested toward the lad.

It therefore caused him great consternation when he learned that Joseph was not, in fact, staying at Mamre.

Night had nearly fallen when Reuben's laborious trek toward camp was interrupted by Gad. Racing up from the field that ran toward the south, Gad hailed him, waving his arms and shouting.

"Asher and I were just bedding down our flocks," he cried as he came upon him. "From the rise we could see the highway, and coming this way a traveler!"

Panting and holding his sides, he caught up with Reuben, who anxiously inquired, "Does he have a large company? We will not give up our place lightly."

"No, no," Gad went on. "That was our concern as well. But when he came closer, we could see that no company followed, and . . . he is not a stranger!"

"I have no time for riddles!" Reuben snapped, and hastening on, headed for camp, supper, and bed.

"You do not understand," Gad replied, grasping him by the sleeve. "It is our brother. It is Joseph who approaches!"

Stopping in his tracks, Reuben studied Gad dubiously. As he absorbed the news, he also noted the scheming gleam in the man's eye.

Before he could question him further, Gad was off, himself heading for camp to break the word to the others.

On his trail came Asher, passing Reuben with an eager stride. The elder brother did not like his expression any better than Gad's.

Whatever the two were up to, he was certain they intended Joseph no good.

* * *

Encumbered with his bulky saddle, which needed to cure after its rubdown, Reuben slowly led his hungry horse toward camp. By the time he reached the others, they had already begun to contrive their wicked plot against Joseph.

"The dreamer is coming!" Gad and Asher had announced.

Quickly the hate-filled minds of the nine brothers colluded and conspired.

As Reuben came upon them, frightening words hissed from their drawn lips, and their bent heads nodded together. Judah stood a little way from the others, but Reuben noted that even he was not objecting to their plans.

"Let's kill him!" someone said. "He will not reach camp until it is fully dark. Even if someone passes on the road, we will never be seen!"

Had it gone so far, their jealousy? Had resentment blossomed into murder? With sweating hands Reuben set his saddle beside his tent and tethered his horse. Carefully he listened to the voices circling the campfire, and his flesh prickled.

Fidgeting with his brown beard, Reuben darted a glance over his shoulder. Vainly he hoped to see Joseph approaching, that he might warn him, that he might rush him away from the would-be assassins.

In fact, he would have turned away to find him, to divert him from the danger, but the brothers had already seen Reuben in the shadows and hailed him.

Quickly he considered his options. He could pretend not to hear them, he could say he left something at the cistern and go in quest of Joseph. But when Joseph did not arrive, they would likely suspect Reuben and come after them both.

No, he had no choice. He must join the jesters at the fire, the laughers with toothy grins and evil designs.

"Lord Jehovah," he whispered. Reuben must handle this very discretely.

Pulling his shoulders back, he pretended nonchalance.

"So, Little One is on his way," he said, approaching his companions with an easy swagger.

"You know?" Naphtali enthused.

"Yes, yes, we told him," Gad announced. "Have you seen him, Reuben?"

"Not yet," the elder laughed, taking a seat. "What's the plan?"

Eagerly they filled his ears. "We've had enough of his bragging!" Dan cried. "He plots to overthrow us, Reuben! Don't you know?"

The elder replied nothing, pretending neither agreement nor surprise at this aberration.

"Next year, when he turns eighteen, he will have menservants of his own," Asher projected, "and after that an army, if he wishes. How shall he force us to bow to him, as he says, without a war!"

"Indeed!" Zebulun joined in. "Shall we sit still while our enemy rises over us? You know he is Jacob's favorite. Anything he asks—soldiers, weapons, even war machines —all will be his!"

Reuben studied his brothers' crazed expressions in the firelight. They had not yet drunk much wine. It was not wine that inspired their maniacal imaginings. It was hate, and the imaginings excused their hatred.

"Let's kill him!" Gad suddenly reasserted, pounding his fist into his thigh and jumping up. His voice, momentarily stunning the others, was followed by cheers and the unsheathing of knives.

"We can cover the deed. No one need know!" he shouted. "We shall cast him into one of the cisterns by the road. We can tell Father a wild beast devoured him!"

"Yes," Asher raved, "then let's see what becomes of his dreams!"

Reuben rose up rigid on his seat. "Brothers, brothers!" he cried, raising his hands. When he had their attention he tempered his tone. "Are you sure this is what you want? Think! Jehovah watches!"

The group, silenced by the rebuke, squirmed angrily.

"Jehovah! Jehovah!" someone objected. "Indeed, he watches. Would he have us hide our heads while Joseph supplants us?"

At this everyone rallied, and cheers rose again.

Losing ground, Reuben turned to Judah. "Brother," he said, trying not to sound desperate, "do you agree with this?"

Uneasy at being singled out, Judah glanced nervously around the group. He was about to reply, but caught by Asher's warning look, he gave a weak smile and only shrugged.

"Of course he agrees!" Gad insisted. "He is a son of the first wife, like you, Reuben! Judah has much to lose!"

At this, Asher leaned close to Gad, whispering in his ear and eyeing Reuben suspiciously. The eldest brother must reconsider his position, and quickly.

Fearing now for his own safety, and knowing that if something happened to him no one could save Joseph, Reuben tried a different tack.

Standing up, he placed a faggot on the fire and casually wiped his hands on his cloak.

"I can see that Father and I have taught you well," he conceded. "You do right to put the interests of your property and your welfare above all else. After all, the protection of your inheritance is a sacred trust."

The brothers, mollified, listened with more respect, muttering to one another and nodding their heads.

Looking over his shoulder again, Reuben still did not see Joseph. Quickly he added, "It is a good idea to throw him into one of the cisterns. But, I say, let us not take his life."

When Gad and Asher started angrily, he repeated, "Shed no blood. Throw him into the pit, but do not lay hands on him, for how do you know but that his blood will be required of you? Then what will all your wise intentions have accomplished?"

If there was one thing on which all the cultures of Canaan and Mesopotamia were agreed, it was that reaping always followed sowing, not only in the natural world, but in the spiritual. Appealing to his brothers' fears of retribution, Reuben had them cornered.

Silence filled the firelit circle for a long moment. Then, at last, Asher rallied.

Hoisting a wineskin, he suddenly declared, "Well said, Reuben! Let the pit pass the judgment! What chance is there that Joseph can survive in a desert pit?"

Encouraged by this reasoning, the others applauded.

"What chance, especially after we are done with him?" Gad hooted.

Raucous laughter resounded through camp, and the wineskin was tippled from hand to hand.

With apprehensive eyes, Reuben gazed across the darkness toward the road. As he had feared, Joseph was coming, drawn like a pathetic moth toward the camp's beckoning fire.

His heart rending, Reuben would have called out to him in warning. But then he observed his brothers' knotted fists and their conspiring faces, and he resisted.

He only hoped he had bought a chance for Joseph, and that he could live with himself if he had failed.

# PART III
## The Castaway

# 16

Sun, like a fist, smote the bottom of the pit.

Joseph could not be sure he was awake. He was not certain he was alive.

The face of the old man, the shepherd of Shechem, came with the sun, not smiting him but passing in and out of his head like a windblown cloud. At first the face hovered above him, then it entered him, through his sealed and swollen eyes.

Somehow, Joseph managed to turn himself from his stomach to his back and lay for a long time face up, the sides of the tall pit enclosing him like a womb.

As consciousness replaced the swoon, so did throbbing pain replace its anesthesia.

Once, when with great effort he opened an eye, he thought the old shepherd sat on the lip of the cistern, his legs dangling over the edge toward him, his face somber but reassuring. When Joseph tried to reach forth a hand, however, the old man vanished—and with him, the hope he inspired.

Crushing pain enveloped the youngster just as the walls enveloped him, but searing him and coursing through him with each laborious pulse of his heart.

His body, which had not yet recovered from his fight in the Hebron hills, and which had endured the hard journey from Mamre to Dothan, had sustained further serious injuries. Could he have seen himself, his churning stomach would have revolted.

Several kicks to the torso had left him with bruised ribs and organs. His head, wounded when he was cast like a barley bag over the cistern's ledge, was distended, a large lump protruding from his brow.

It must be noontime, he considered. It was his first fully alert thought. The sun was directly above the cistern, and though it was wintertime, the pit captured the rays and held them against the dry bottom, wringing from them all the warmth they could provide.

Fever tormented Joseph, and he hated the sun. Vainly he tried to shield his face, but he could not raise a hand to do so.

Resigned, insofar as resignation or any act of will was possible, Joseph accepted that he would die here.

The swoon was about to reclaim him when a dull rumble reached his ears.

At first he felt that his head would burst—that the phantom sound was the rush of angels' wings, and that it heralded the coming of the end. But as reality again imposed itself upon him, he interpreted the roar more clearly.

Through the haze of growing consciousness he remembered that the pit was beside a highway and that it was a stopping place for caravans. Still unable to move, he let the sound of horses' hooves and churning wheels sweep over him.

As the company, enormous by the sound of it, came to a halt, and the rumble tapered to shouts and commands, Joseph vaguely recognized that the voices spoke an Arabian tongue. He cared not who they were or what nation they were of. He only hoped someone might glance into the dry cistern and see him, for no worse evil could befall him than he had already endured.

He must have groaned. Somehow, through his pain and his need, his soul found its voice, and he moaned loudly enough to be heard.

Momentarily, faces peered over the side of the pit—

brown faces, covered by desert dust or concealed by dingy white veils. Turbaned heads shook and nodded as the amazed caravaneers spied the source of the peculiar sound.

Then the men disappeared, and Joseph wondered if they were a vision, like the shepherd of Shechem.

But he could hear them now, conferring beyond the pit, rattling in their strange tongue.

Then another rumbling, as of a second caravan, could be discerned. Joseph could not tell north from south, trapped as he was. But it was apparent that this new train would converge upon the first from the opposite direction.

Suddenly the Arabians were more vocal, trading ideas back and forth and staring into the pit at Joseph as though he were a commodity and not a man.

Finding a remnant of strength, the son of Jacob managed to lift a hand, pleading for help. But the faces above were not sympathetic.

Were he capable of terror in his weakened state he would have been terrified as he caught a few familiar fragments of their conversation. "Ishmaelites," he heard them say, "Egypt." These words were universal to all languages of the area. And for a Jacobite, these words were cause for fear. For the Ishmaelites had long been enemies of the Jacobites, ever since Great-grandfather Abraham had blessed Isaac over his firstborn, Ishmael. And Egypt was an alien land, its thirteenth and fourteenth dynasties fond of taking Hebrew slaves.

He did not know what the men above the cistern had in mind for him as the second caravan approached. But he was alert enough to be apprehensive.

As the Arabians lowered a rope into the pit, sending one of their strongest after him, Joseph retreated to the sanctuary of unconsciousness.

Like a tabernacle it enveloped him, giving dark at noonday, and quiet oblivion to his fevered soul.

# 17

The flying hooves of Reuben's horse left an angry wake across the desert. Rising like a cumulous cloud, the dust raged, following his eastward trail.

From the fields of the Jacobites Reuben fled, seeking the cisterns and his younger brother, seeking one last chance to save him.

Just this morning, the nine conspirators, who had frolicked the night away in celebration of their victory, had laid yet another design against Joseph. From the site of their breakfast fire, which faced north, they had spied the caravan of the Ishmaelites, the second caravan to approach Joseph's pit. They had not seen the first, the one from the south, which was manned by Midianite Arabs. But the second had sparked their greed.

To Reuben's horror, it was Judah who contrived the plot. He could scarcely believe that his closest brother, the secondborn of Jacob, should stoop so low.

"What profit is it to us to let Joseph die in the pit?" Judah had asked, studying the great train that descended from Gilead. "What do we gain by slaying Joseph and trying to hide the fact? Come, let us sell him to the Ishmaelites."

At first, Asher had rankled at the idea. Murder, or at least the chance that the pit would claim Joseph, was his foremost desire. But as Judah continued his smooth talk the possibility of turning a profit became more attractive.

"As Reuben says, we should not kill our brother," Judah craftily reasoned. "We should spare him. After all, he *is* our own flesh and blood."

That Judah should use Reuben's own words to this end was unpardonable.

At the foot of the firepit lay Joseph's coat, an object of mocking hilarity all through the evening. Before roughing up the lad, the brothers had stripped him of his prize possession, the symbol of his heritage. They had kept it for themselves, passing it back and forth, wearing it and sporting in it all night.

Suddenly, Reuben could conceal his love for Joseph no longer. Caring not what risk it entailed, he leapt to his feet, grasping the coat to himself and racing from the camp.

Across the desert he sped, hoping to reach the cistern before the Ishmaelites did. He knew the brothers would be on his heels. He knew they would be hastening to intervene. But nothing mattered any longer except Joseph's life.

At the sight of the oasis, as he came over the rise on his stamping horse, Reuben's heart raced with hope. The Ishmaelites were already past the place, heading south, and the other caravan, which he had not expected to see, was done with its stop and was moving north.

By the time the brothers arrived, there would be no one to whom they might sell Joseph.

Eagerly he headed toward the pit—the one which only last night had been the scene of the grisly thrashing, the site of the horrible casting away.

In his hand he clasped Joseph's coat, ready to wrap him in it, ready to tenderly return him to his rightful station.

But as he drew near, the sound of his brothers' horses even now echoing from behind, a new fear filled him. What if the caravaneers had found Joseph? What if they had, for some reason, looked into the pit, and seeing him, had stolen him away?

Dread, like a noose, strangled him as he leapt from his mount and ran the last way to the cistern.

Leaning over, he found that the floor was indeed vacant. Little pools of dried blood were the only evidence of the lad's suffering.

Madly he surveyed the road and the retreating clouds of the dust-raising trains. And like a drunkard, he staggered across the desert.

Judah, coming upon him, was followed close by Gad and Asher. Snarling, they glared down at him. But he had no heart for their disappointment.

Defeated, he fell to his face before them, before his failure, before Jehovah.

And holding his hands to the sky, he wept, "The lad is gone! And I . . . where shall I go?"

# 18

The crunch and jolt of wagon wheels awakened Joseph. For a long while he lay dazed and still, wondering where he was.

Above him spread an opaque tarp, so heavy that no light and little air were admitted. Beneath him were bags of grain, as comfortable a bed as he had known since leaving Mamre.

It seemed he was a child again, six years old, and that he was hidden away in Leah's wagon. Any moment he would hear Dinah's voice beside him and feel her tugging on his arm.

Were he to rise up and peek from beneath the tarp, he would surely see the retreating hills of Gilead and his brothers' horses splashing through Jabbok ford.

Jacob would find him in the morning and would speak to him of the angel and the pain in his thigh.

But as he snuggled against the barley bags, he was himself in pain. Gradually the memory of his brothers' fists and kicking blows replaced his dream.

Also, he remembered the fearsome words spoken by his Arabian captors. He knew, now, that he was the unwilling property of whomever had placed him in this wagon.

He found he was able, this time, to move his hand. He was about to raise the tarp where daylight etched a bright line along the wagon rail, but just as his palsied fingers grasped the edge of the heavy fabric, the wagon came to a halt and the voices of the caravaneers filled the morning.

Lowering his hand, he lay very still and listened intently to their unintelligible tongue, hoping to catch a phrase here and there that would tell him more about them.

He did not expect the dramatic way in which his hope would be fulfilled.

Suddenly the tarp was flung back, and crisp sunlight spilled over him. As he turned his head from the glare a shadow fell across him, and he stared into the dark features of a leering Arabian.

"Allah be praised!" the man laughed. "He is still alive!"

The word "Allah," alone, was familiar to Joseph. But it was sufficient to answer many of his questions.

He knew now that his first captors had sold him to the Ishmaelite caravan which met them at the cistern. He also knew that his new owners could have nothing good in mind for him, probably intending to sell him as a slave when they reached Egypt. Such a fate had befallen many Hebrews separated from their tribes.

He also knew that if these men learned he was Jacobite, he might not live to see the borders of Egypt.

It was not so long before, in the scheme of history, that Great-grandfather Abraham had preferred Isaac to his firstborn, Ishmael, bestowing upon Isaac the patriarchal blessing and the greater part of the inheritance. For the Ishmaelite Arabs, the memory of that affront would never die, and any descendant of Isaac was considered an enemy.

Therefore, although Joseph's head was still foggy with delirium, he was wise enough to keep silent.

Reaching into the wagon, the big fellow who stared in at him poked and prodded him as a woman pokes a piece of meat at market.

With a wince, Joseph pulled away, and the man grinned, calling out some crudity to his friends. Hollow laughter met the remark, and soon the wagon was surrounded by other mocking faces.

In a round of gibberish, the men began to question their captive. But Joseph could not answer them, for he did not know the language. As they persisted, however, the big man pointed to his companions, calling out their names one by one and indicating that Joseph was to introduce himself.

Refusing to cooperate, he replied, "Call me Hebrew."

"Hebrew?" the man snarled. "Habiru!" he laughed, turning to his friends, and repeating the word in their tongue. Everyone laughed again, but as Joseph continued to deny a name, claiming his lifestyle as his only identity, they grew sullen.

Suddenly the leering fellow grasped at Joseph's tunic and pulled him to a sitting position. Patting him on the cheek, he bared his yellow teeth and breathed warm garlic into Joseph's face.

Directing him to look over the wagon's edge, he pointed an angry finger toward the horizon.

"Egypt!" he growled.

How long Joseph had lain semiconscious in the wagon, he did not know, but it was at least a month by caravan from Dothan to the borders of Egypt. To the youngster's amazement, the distant line of earth against sky was marked with a jagged wall, enormous, snakelike, designating the boundary of the greatest nation under heaven.

The Land of the Nile lay straight ahead—the sanctuary of the shepherds, the sons of Isaac, having faded with the desert far behind.

As the lad sat stunned on the barley bags, his captor, who appeared to be the train's yeoman, began shouting commands. Soon men were scattering, running for water, rags, and fresh clothes.

Placing his large hands under Joseph's arms, the yeoman lifted him from the wagon and stood him on his feet. Like a newborn calf, Joseph buckled, his legs weak as butter. But the Arab began to walk him about, forcing him to use his atrophied limbs.

At last, he took him to the shade of a small tent, and clapping his hands, called for a servant girl.

Deftly, the young woman began to wash the dirt and encrusted blood from Joseph's arms and legs. He would have resisted when she pulled his tunic over his head, leaving him in his loincloth. But the Arab was close by, and Joseph must submit.

He must submit likewise as she attended to his blood-matted hair. The lustrous dark locks must be cut, and soon a razor worked even at his disheveled beard.

Between the tentflaps Joseph could see the wall of Egypt, formidable, irresistible. As he studied it, his heart shivering, the razor sheared him like a sheep.

It was a shame to be shaven, the mark of a slave.

But freedom was his no longer. He had lost it at Dothan to the will of his brothers, to the will of his brothers' God.

# 19

Like a bloody finger, the red granite obelisk of On pierced the afternoon sky. Flies buzzed through the busy marketplace, tormenting the queue of naked captives who stood in the obelisk's shadow.

It was never wintertime in Egypt. Here, except for morning and afternoon thunderstorms, the season was hot. Joseph, who stood with his hands bound behind him, inched forward with the queue, his eyes locked upon the auction block where soon he would be standing. Sweat poured in rivulets down his bare torso, soaking his striped loincloth, the only garment allowed him.

He would have given an arm to just once swat at the pestering flies diving at his head. But he had no right over his own body.

His scalp burned, exposed to the sun for the first time since infancy. Shorn of his heavy hair and of his lustrous beard, the tender skin was readily inflamed. As he moved out of the obelisk's shadow, he cringed.

On was the first major city to which the Ishmaelite caravan had come upon entering Egypt. The capital of Egyptian science and knowledge, the magnificent city was also the religious center of the empire, devoted to the chief god, Ra, god of the sun.

Joseph had often heard of the great monolith whose shadow stretched the length of the central avenue. The obelisk represented all that was Egyptian, from worship to government. In effect its shadow reached from end to end of the Nile Valley.

For Joseph, however, as for any Israelite, the monolith was a repugnant sight, a symbol of the bewildering paganism which characterized this mightiest of nations.

The auction tent, spread through the middle of On's central square, was the chief attraction of the marketplace. Its enormous striped awning sheltered countless bales, casks, bolts, cartons, and barrels of goods.

The Arabian caravan that had brought Joseph to this land had been laden with flasks of balm, myrrh, and gum resin, all procured in Gilead. The costly products would sell for a high price in this bazaar.

Joseph wearily surveyed the marketplace. Visions of Mamre, of the verdant oaks and the clean stream that fed them, drifted through his mind, weighing him with sadness. Against a wall across the plaza stood the yeoman of the caravan, his hefty arms crossed over his chest as he waited for his most valuable possession to be auctioned.

The young Hebrew was a rare find, and though the Arab had paid dearly for him, giving the Midianites a full week's wages, the strong young man would bring a handsome price today.

True, Joseph was not in the finest shape. Bruised and debilitated, he did not make as good a showing as he might. But the reserve price placed on his head took this into account, and anyone considering the purchase could see by Joseph's physique and well-turned muscles that he was a good risk.

Throughout the trip to Egypt, the yeoman had seen to it that the captive was kept alive, fed, and nursed, at last, to consciousness.

Joseph had been bathed and his worst wounds were anointed with healing balm. Already the lad was reviving beneath the warming sun, color overcoming the deadly pallor that had been his. The yeoman eagerly licked his lips, savoring the scent of money.

As for Joseph himself, he felt anything but strong. His

knees were wobbly, he sweltered beneath the sun's caress, and each forward step required increasing effort.

"Lord Jehovah," he whispered under his breath, "God of Abraham, Isaac, and Jacob..."

The auction platform was now directly before him. He would be the next one called forth.

Shame filled him and he kept his naked head bowed even as one of the auction assistants bent over to unshackle his ankles. But when yet another assistant grasped Joseph rudely by the arm, leading him to the block, rebellion suddenly surged through him, flooding him with adrenaline. Wrenching free, he wheeled about, striking the man with his two bound fists and throwing him off balance.

Stunned, the man fell back against the platform, and his partner, racing to help him, left Joseph standing free in front of the onlooking crowd.

Pandemonium broke loose in the marketplace, as Joseph's fellow captives took his lead, and rising up in kind, began to push through the throng, kicking their shackled feet and winding like a formidable chain toward the avenue.

With instant camaraderie, the captives—black Nubians from Ethiopia, pale-skinned barbarians from Europe, and olive-complected Semites of many tribes—forged ahead, upsetting business and terrifying those who stood in their way.

In ripple effect, the disturbance at the auction tent spread through the bazaar. Joseph, although the instigator, found attention distracted from himself and within moments was mingling anonymously with the frenzied crowd.

Working his way toward the back wall of the marketplace, he thought to find an exit, and once free, would seek escape. The fact that his hands were bound behind him was an inconvenience he could not correct just now.

Sidling through the press he found that the market ended only yards from the monoliths' broad base. Behind the obelisk was the gate to the Temple of Ra, portal to the city's acropolis and to the sanctuaries of government.

The Gate of On, main entrance to the city, lay a short distance beyond, and like an arrow he aimed for it.

Just as he did so, however, he was grabbed from behind and thrown to the ground, his face scraping the pavement.

Two hundred pounds of human flesh held him down, the Arabian caravaneer having once again captured him, and sitting now upon his back.

"So, you thought to rob me!" the Ishmaelite snarled, his words lost on Joseph. "Come!"

Grasping the youngster by the wrists, he wrenched him up from the ground, sending shooting pains through the captive's shoulders. Then turning Joseph to face him, he began to slap him, holding him by one hand and buffeting him with the other.

The people near the gate were joined by the crowd from the marketplace, which, unruly and loud, spurred the yeoman's vengeance. And when the human chain of shackled prisoners, so far unrestrained, approached the gate, they found their hero in sorrier condition than ever.

The caravaneer would likely have beaten his slave to death, had a new character not entered the scene.

The bloodthirsty crowd was reveling in revenge when suddenly a hush came over it. Those people closest to the temple were the first to grow quiet, and as they quieted, they bowed themselves to the ground.

Row upon row, the reverence spread, as a dignitary of some importance descended the temple steps. Soon his name was passing from whisper to whisper.

"Potiphera . . ." some said, while others used the nickname, "Potiphar . . ." The word obviously evoked awe, and soon everyone about the caravaneer and the captive was prostrate upon the ground.

The yeoman, recognizing that this newcomer merited obeisance, likewise bowed down, still holding Joseph firmly by the wrists.

Trumpets blared from the temple steps and one of the dignitary's numerous attendants announced his entrance.

"Potiphera, Priest of On, High Priest of Ra, Captain of the Sacred Bodyguard! All bow! Humble yourselves before His Reverence!"

Over and over the announcement was heralded as Potiphera made his way to the street.

Joseph, standing in the middle of the avenue, dusty and sweat-streaked, momentarily forgot his struggle as the auspicious gentleman drew near. Flanked on each side by attendants—scribes, valets, accountants, and counselors—and followed by spear-bearing guards, Potiphera was a striking figure. Joseph was head and shoulders taller than many of the men in the crowd, but Potiphera equaled him for stature. And the fine strands of silver that wound through his banded goatee added grace and dignity to his appearance.

Garbed in a tight body tunic which reached to his knees, Potiphera was royally attired. His headdress was a helmet, reserved for nobility of the highest class, and upon his neck and descending toward his breast was a broad collar of lacquered plates, edged in gold.

The most outstanding feature of his garb was the emblem that adorned both his headdress and his collar, a wide ornament shaped like falcon wings spreading out from a golden circle. From each side of the circle two snakeheads protruded, likewise of lacquer and gold. This ornament Joseph recognized as the winged sun-disk, symbol of the sun-god, Ra.

His wrists still gripped tight in the yeoman's hand, Joseph studied the priest with wide eyes. Like the rest of the onlookers, he was riveted by Potiphera's quiet glory, but unlike them, he did not bow.

Perhaps it was this that drew Potiphera's attention. Perhaps it was the fact that the priest had observed the scuffle in the street only moments before.

Whatever it was that captured his focus, Potiphera paused before the lad, surveying him with a bemused expression.

Up and down he eyed him, saying nothing, while the crowd grew restless and the yeoman apprehensive.

When at last the Ishmaelite got courage to peer up at the priest, he met with disapproval. Without a word, Potiphera persuaded him to release his grip on the youngster.

"Unbind him!" Potiphera commanded.

The yeoman stammered and stuttered, but Potiphera did not repeat himself.

At last, the Ishmaelite complied and, chagrined, he stepped aside.

Now the priest drew closer to Joseph. "Who are you?" he asked, using the Egyptian dialect which was the language of commerce familiar to all but the most ignorant of foreigners.

Joseph pulled himself up straight and tall, rubbing his throbbing wrists. "I am Hebrew," he answered.

The yeoman laughed nervously. "Yes, yes . . . this is all he will tell you," he said, fearing the captive would offend the priest and call down further disfavor on both their heads.

But the priest, ignoring the yeoman, continued to study Joseph.

"Are you the source of disquiet in my city this day?" he inquired.

Of course he must have known the answer to that question, having been informed of the upset in the marketplace and of the upstart slave who had instigated it.

Joseph did not reply, refusing to accommodate the Egyptian.

The yeoman, fidgeting uneasily, was ready to intercede, but Potiphera silenced him with a glance.

Standing back, the priest walked around Joseph, and as he did, a smile worked at his face.

Then, turning to his attendants, he nodded. "We must deal with this rebel. He must be taught compliance."

"Yes, sir," one of the soldiers agreed, snapping to attention. Coming toward Joseph, he intended to haul him off to prison, but Potiphera shook his head.

"No, no," he sighed. "Handle him gently, and pay the auctioneer a fair price. The best way to keep an eye on this Hebrew is to take him home."

Bewildered, the soldier shrugged. "Your Highness, you mean..."

"Yes," Potiphera replied, and looking down at the Ishmaelite, "he is still for sale, is he not?"

The yeoman shot a quick glance at the slave. "Why, of course, Your Lordship. And a good price I will give you!"

"Very well," the priest said, and leaving the details to his accountants, he passed down the avenue without a second thought.

# 20

Glorious sunset, mauve and tangerine, lit the servants' court of Potiphera's house. It spilled in deepening shades through the open ceiling, reflecting off the scrubbed white of the limestone walls and strangely affecting Joseph's spirit.

He should have been miserable. He had just been hauled to the auction block of a slave market, had failed in his courageous attempt to save himself, and had been purchased, like chattel, by a pagan priest.

He was another man's property—the property of a heathen foreigner—and he had no rights, being less than a dog in Egyptian society. Indeed, among the pantheon of this bewildering empire, the dog was worshiped, as was most every animal that walked, crawled, or slithered across the earth.

Men and women, captured and enslaved, were less than human, less than the dogs or snakes or vermin to whom temples were erected and sacrifices offered.

Despite his situation, Joseph was strangely satisfied by the violet and vermilion of the night.

Little had been expected of him since he had been introduced to the house. He had in fact been allowed to recline in the servants' quarters upon the couch where he now sat, until his sorely depleted strength returned.

And he had already been fed more than once on fare both nutritious and exotic.

Potiphera had seen to it that he was treated kindly.

Joseph did not know why he was thus dealt with, but he did not question it, having little strength for deep thinking.

He did sense, when he pondered anything, that Jehovah was with him. And he sensed that this strange Potiphera, pagan though he was, could somehow be the instrument of God Almighty.

He shivered, drawing up his shoulders as he considered his powerless condition. Though the reality of it would take a long time dawning, the very thought of enslavement horrified him.

But then the russet light soothed him, calling to him from beyond the wall like the whisper of the Lord, caressing him like Rachel's hand, and upholding him like the voice of Jacob.

How long he sat upon the couch, silently observing the bustle of the kitchen hands and listening to the soft chatter of the maids, he did not know. The workers who went about their business in the court were of various classes. Those in charge were hired servants. Under them were indentured servants, each one designated by a silver post placed in a small hole bored through the left earlobe. Then there were the slaves, marked by brands upon their necks. But what struck Joseph was that, despite these outward emblems, everyone worked peaceably together. Even the slaves were accorded unusual respect.

Joseph's attention was attracted to one fellow in particular, who was apparently the kitchen manager. The Hebrew was intrigued by him, not only because he ran his affairs as chief baker with efficiency and authority, but also because his left ear bore the mark of the awl. Although he no longer wore a small silver post through the lobe, which all of the other indentured workers wore, there was a hole—a sure sign that this man had once owed his life to the master.

Why he would have continued in service to Potiphera, once having earned his freedom, Joseph could not imagine. But with dexterity and joy he ran the kitchen, and now and then, as he bent over the breadboard and joined his underlings in their mundane activities, a song or a merry whistle spilled from his throat.

Bald as a desert dune he was, round as a pumpkin; and his cheeks were like pomegranates, red and full. His servants and slaves called him by name, Phineas. But though the name was Egyptian, he did not have the lank body and narrow nose of the race.

Joseph studied him for a long while, cheered by his presence just as the others were, and he wondered about him.

Dark was coming on. As it did, the pace of the kitchen work increased. The grand meal of the day in Egyptian society was reserved for late evening. Several times Phineas clapped his hands, spurring his workers. It was time to serve the food. Trays of copper and silver, containing roast partridge, enormous honey rolls, and piles of succulent figs and olives, were carried into the dining room.

Joseph could not see this room as it lay beyond a narrow, curtain-covered portal. He could, however, imagine the activity of the chamber, as couches were arranged about low tables and golden goblets were filled with the first round of wine.

No one had yet arrived for the feast, but anticipation was in the air. Every night was banquet night in Potiphera's house, as the evening meal was a time of entertaining the endless stream of dignitaries who came to call.

None of the grand folk who frequented the residence could have impressed the young Hebrew slave more than Phineas, however. As he observed him, the plump fellow suddenly wheeled about, surveying the kitchen for any forgotten details. When he did, his eyes fell upon the newcomer, and his expression, already jovial, softened warmly.

"Hebrew?" he called across the room.

"Yes, sir," the slave replied, straightening his weary shoulders.

"You will help serve tonight," he commanded. "Look sharp now!"

Joseph stood up from the couch and cleared his throat. "Serve, sir?" he marveled. "But, I do not know..."

"You will learn quickly enough. Stay at my elbow and follow my instructions."

With this, Phineas motioned him forward and folded a pristine linen towel over his left arm. As he looked him over, turning him about, he shook his head and sighed.

"Madam arrives tonight...any moment I'm sure. She will be bringing a gaggle of fine ladies. Keep quiet and you will do well."

With that, he directed Joseph to follow him through the portal, where he would explain the details of the feast.

When Joseph entered the chamber, he was surprised by the feminine decor of the tables. Pink lilies from the Nile mixed in profusion with purple irises and red garden roses, all arranged like glorious bushes in ornate vases about the room. Muscular Nubian menservants, their dark skin oiled until it glistened, held ostrich-feather fans in each corner, adding a visual accent which would have pleased any woman's eye.

In this setting, Phineas, who had commandeered the kitchen, took a secondary role, deferring instantly to a tall thin man who bore himself with austere pride.

His eyes cold as spearpoints, the haughty one approached Phineas and scrutinized his charge.

"Is this the Hebrew?" he snapped.

"Yes," Phineas replied. "Is he not pleasing?"

The man, who was governor of the feast, walked

around Joseph two or three times, and at last sniffed disdainfully.

"Madam will be pleased," he conceded. "That is what matters."

# 21

Potiphera had one weakness. In all other matters he was a man of dignity: clearheaded, devoutly spiritual and keen witted. But in this one area, he could be as addle-pated as a schoolboy.

His single blindspot was his ravishing wife, Natira.

After 20 years of marriage, he was as smitten by her as the day his father, the previous high priest, had brought her before him.

Potiphera indulged Natira at every opportunity. No wish she might have was too great for him to grant, no whim too frivolous. He even anticipated her desires, seeking to fulfill them before she asked.

Thus it was that the priest had purchased the young Hebrew slave.

Natira had a penchant for handsome young men. She surrounded herself with them, possessing so many male valets and personal servants that her husband might have questioned her motivation.

But Potiphera never questioned; his trust of Natira was nearly childlike.

Tonight he stood in the entryway of his home, awaiting his wife's arrival. She had been in the imperial capital of Memphis for three weeks, visiting in Pharaoh's palace. This evening she would be returning and would be bringing with her a host of royal ladies who would guest in the priest's home.

Their visit would culminate in the arrival of Pharaoh

himself, and his queen, who would take up residence in the king's winter palace for his annual stay in On.

Situated somewhat inland from the Nile, On was less humid and less chilly than Memphis this time of year. For royalty pampered by the mildest of climates, slight variation in temperature was cause for relocation, and the priest's house had become a haven.

In fact, so connected was Potiphera's estate with the royal compound of On that the two were considered by the general populace as one property.

The priest leaned through the large door of his estate, looking eagerly down the cobbled boulevard. Rewarded by the sound of carriage wheels, he stepped onto the porch, smoothing his lavender tunic and stroking his crimped beard.

Ascending the main avenue to the acropolis was a stunning parade of horsedrawn cabs, glittering with gold and burnished by the rosy twilight. Within moments they lined the drive of Potiphera's mansion, and an even more stunning array of ladies emerged.

Perfumed and perfected by cosmetics, decked in a profusion of silks and jewels, the women formed a fluttery processional, descending upon Potiphera and his home like a flock of exotic birds.

The ladies were more alike than individual. Devoted to fashion, these high-society females strove for the thin look, denying themselves rich foods until they conformed to the body-hugging designs dictated for their gowns.

Paper-thin sandals adorned their feet, designed more for appearance than for practicality. Slender laces crisscrossed up their calves to emphasize the length of their legs.

The dresses they wore were simple but elegant— sarong-like and gathered at one shoulder, leaving the other bare. Whites and pastels dominated, allowing each woman's personal expression to radiate in her jewels.

Gaudy gold and silver ornaments were layered about the women's necks, and spectacular arm bands, anklets, and bracelets balanced the effect.

Delicate scarves trailed from waists, wrists, and necks; or were held lightly in the fingers and dragged carelessly upon the pavement as though they had not cost their husbands' budgets dearly.

But in each case the crowning touch was the coiffure.

Most of the women wore wigs, all in the perfectly black color so admired by their class. Any female blessed with naturally straight hair could forego a wig, though she must use dye to match the ebony she craved.

The hairstyle of the day was starkly streamlined, bluntly cut but meticulously woven here and there with jeweled braids or crimped curls.

Cosmetics were used liberally, porcelain complexions accented by ruby lips and heavily lined eyes. Mascara and charcoal were applied unsparingly, drawn along the eyelids and brought out toward the temples in winglike streaks.

Potiphera watched the parade with masculine appreciation, but his eyes favored Natira, leader of the flock.

Though this grand lady possessed an enviably thin waist and narrow hips, she was buxom as a Nile barge and did not quite fit the twig-like figure stipulated by the fashion powers. If she was proud of her well-endowed torso, it was because she knew what men liked, and what men liked did not always conform to trend.

Whenever Potiphera watched Natira walk, he was swept up on her movements, his heart helplessly carried like a leaf on a graceful wave. After 20 years he was still so affected, still so in love.

As she approached him this evening, her companions laughing and gossiping through the door, she paused. Lightly she stroked his face, running her scented fingers through his beard.

She said not a word, however, focusing on him only briefly and then hurrying off to attend to her guests.

Behind her trailed a younger woman, tall like Natira, but more slender. Quietly, she too paused before Potiphera, awaiting his attention.

With a sigh, the man at last entered the house, his eyes following his wife as she disappeared down the hall. He did not immediately acknowledge the younger lady's presence.

"Papa," the girl whispered, touching him lightly on the sleeve.

"Asenath!" he exclaimed. "I did not see you!"

The girl shook her head, laughing gently. "Surely you know by now," she teased, "I am never far from Mother's shadow."

Potiphera embraced the girl fondly, pressing his cheek to her silky hair.

"No, no," the priest corrected. "You are a child of the Sun. Shadow does not become you."

# 22

From the kitchen door, Phineas, the chief baker, watched his new slave fulfill his duties at the banquet. The young Hebrew was proving himself surprisingly adequate for the task, and the baker, knowing the striking lad had spent his life as a nomad, wondered how he could circulate so capably in this setting.

Proceeding from table to table, Joseph filled wine goblets and saw to it that the platters and bowls of food were kept hot and fresh. If he now and then showed a sign of nervousness, or forgot to serve from a guest's right side, the diners were not offended, charmed as they were by his quiet manner and his ruddy good looks.

For this was a women's banquet. Potiphera had turned the dining room over to Natira for the evening, and all of the ladies were enthralled by the handsome youngster with the night-dark eyes.

The chief baker did not know that Joseph had much experience as a servant. Despite the fact that he was a tribal prince, Joseph had often filled his father's cup at dinner, and had learned early how to fetch and carry for his elder brothers.

Then too, the chief baker could not know that Jacob had instilled in his son an abiding respect for women, never allowing a superior attitude toward Dinah, Leah, Rachel, or the concubines.

If Joseph appeared to move easily in this setting, however, it was not due to confidence on his part, or to lack of anxiety. The baker did not see that Joseph's hands sweated, or that he sometimes stammered when addressed.

Natira, of course, basked in the reception her new slave evoked. "Where did you get him?" her friends marveled. "Isn't he adorable!"

The hostess knew he was a favor from Potiphera, a homecoming gift, and she proudly told her guests so.

The notion shamed Joseph, who understood enough of the language they spoke to be appalled. But he did not show his feelings and kept his head bowed when he came to Natira's table.

Natira's table. The long, low ebony piece dominated the chamber, its crisp linen cover contrasting starkly with the gleaming veneer. The mistress, her skin as white as the linen, her hair as black as the ebony, reclined behind it like a peacock at rest.

When Joseph drew near to fill her cup, she nodded her head, the plume of azure feathers which adorned her coiffure waving to him solicitously.

The young man's heart surged, but not with admiration. In Natira's presence he felt only fear, as though she were very powerful and very dangerous.

In vain did he keep his eyes lowered. She bored through him with her gaze, her slender arm serpentine as she held forth her goblet.

Ascending from her wrist, up the curve of her forearm, was a golden snake, inset with rubies and emeralds. Like a beckoning finger it compelled his eyes to travel toward her face.

Studying the pitcher in his hand, he resisted, and moved on to the next lady.

"Thank you," a soft voice said as he finished pouring the neighbor's cup.

Struck by the kind tone, Joseph turned toward the voice and stood in stunned silence. Reclined upon the couch beside Natira's was another beauty, the image of the grand lady, only younger, more innocent.

Joseph was motionless, his pitcher poised upright in his hand. While he stared into this lady's eyes, a twitter of giggles passed about the hall. He did not hear them, focusing only on the Egyptian girl.

It was not until his mistress, Natira, called out to him that he lurched alert.

"Hebrew!" she barked. "You have not told us your name." Then, demurring, she recast her approach. "Please honor us with your name."

Natira was leaning toward him, her painted face insistent. Joseph knew it was not customary to introduce a slave to one's guests. Nor could he imagine the woman's purpose.

He would have kept the secret forever, never revealing a single thing about himself. But the younger woman was watching him.

"Joseph," he said before he knew it. "My name is Joseph."

It was to the younger lady that he spoke, as though she and not his owner had inquired.

This affront would not go unnoticed. Rising up on her couch, Natira studied the insolent slave with dagger eyes.

The giggle which had a moment ago filled the room, turned to disapproving murmurs. Joseph had crossed the sacred line of Natira's disfavor, and he would not readily be forgiven.

# 23

Joseph entered the kitchen, his pitcher still clutched in his hand and his throat dry. The Egyptian girl filled his mind, so that he hardly noticed his manager, Phineas, hunched in the corner.

Bent over the chubby fellow was the governor of the feast, the chief butler, his long, angular face contorted viciously. Joseph did not catch a syllable that passed between the two, but when the butler turned on him, he knew he was the cause of their conflict.

"Fetch him!" the man snarled, pointing Phineas toward the Hebrew.

With this, the plump baker hastened to Joseph, leading him across the room, shaking his head and clucking his tongue.

"Not good. Not good," he sighed. "Tophet is very angry. Madam is very angry. Master Potiphera would be angry if he knew."

"What is it, sir?" Joseph asked. "Have I offended?"

"You have insulted our lady!" Tophet replied, grabbing Joseph from Phineas and pushing him into the corner. "Who are you to ignore the mistress when she addresses you?"

"I . . . I did not mean . . ." Joseph stammered.

"You did not mean," Tophet mocked. "Phineas will see to it that you think more clearly in the future. Right, Phineas?"

The baker's eyes were wide in his round face. But the butler was insistent. "Yes, Phineas, he is your charge. You

must put the brand upon his neck. Perhaps it will burn
through to the cobwebs in his brain!"

The butler's hands were like narrow vises on Joseph's
arms. The young Hebrew could have shaken himself
free, but there was nowhere to run.

He knew what Tophet meant by "the brand." He had
seen the ugly scars upon the throats of the kitchen slaves.
Already he could feel the searing poker on his flesh and
smell the burning of his skin.

Fear surged through him and he wrenched in the
butler's grip. Phineas darted a compassionate glance at
his fevered face and shook his head in warning.

"Steady, lad," he whispered. "You make matters
worse..."

"Quiet!" Tophet growled. "Always you have too much
compassion. Save your sympathy for yourself. You must
soon answer to Madam for this Hebrew's behavior!"

* * *

Phineas gently wiped a yellow salve upon Joseph's
branded neck, tears streaming down his cheeks as he did
so. "I am sorry, so sorry," he wept, his voice husky and
soft. "I had no choice, you must understand."

Joseph cringed with pain, wanting to shield the wound
upon his throat, but Phineas pulled his hand away. "Let
the salve do its work," he cautioned. "If you touch the
brand it will become festered."

On the floor, the poker with the burning brand smoked
and sizzled. Joseph studied it in horror.

"It is the sign of the sun!" he rasped, referring to the
rayed symbol which throbbed red hot on its tip. "I do not
worship the sun!"

Phineas knelt before the chair where Joseph sat, his
expression full of feeling. "Does it really matter? You are
Potiphera's slave now."

"It matters!" Joseph cried.

Phineas looked over his shoulder, as if to be sure they were alone on the kitchen veranda. It was very late, and the household servants had retired.

"I know it matters," he sighed, speaking freely. "I know who you are."

Joseph's eyes swam with tears, the brand pulsing mercilessly in his flesh. "You know my name," he groaned. "That is all."

"I know that you are a son of Jacob, the Israelite. Need I know more?"

The slave winced. "How have you learned this?" he marveled.

"I have been with Potiphera only a few years," the baker explained. "I have mastered the Egyptian tongue and have received a new name. But I am Hebrew like you."

Joseph surveyed him through bleary eyes. "Hebrew?" he whispered.

"A servant of Edom," Phineas confessed.

"Edomite?" the lad cried. "A member of Esau's tribe!"

The baker hushed him quickly, looking about again. "This shall be our secret, yours and mine," he cautioned. "It shall be our secret that we both worship Jehovah."

# 24

Joseph stood on the mezzanine of Potiphera's mansion, watching the rearranging of furniture on the court floor. At Tophet's insistence, he had worked for days in close quarters with Phineas, and had not been allowed to leave the kitchen except to sleep in his corner of the servants' chamber. It was refreshing to observe the activity of the larger world.

Strewn about the patio were recent market purchases. The young Hebrew was dazzled by the array of luxurious goods: bolts of colorful silks and tapestries, stashes of fancy baskets and copper vessels, casks of incense and vases of ornamental plumes. Amidst this profusion the furniture was being pushed and shoved as the housekeepers quibbled over the best arrangement.

"Well, what do you think?" Phineas laughed, joining Joseph on the balcony. "All this so that Madam may entertain in style! Every year it is this way. Just before Pharaoh arrives, she stocks the larders, hangs new curtains, reupholsters every couch, and replaces every dish in the house."

"Pharaoh Timaeus is coming here?" Joseph asked in amazement.

"As he does annually," Phineas replied. Then, smirking, he nodded toward the doorway across the court. Tophet had just emerged from the dining hall, gesturing nervously to the servants who scooted tables and lounges across the floor. "Over here, no over there," he commanded, directing a dozen people in a dozen different directions. "Oh, do be careful!"

But Joseph was still in awe of the baker's news.

"Pharaoh, here?" he marveled. "Have you ever seen him? What is he like?"

"He is Theban," Phineas answered cryptically, as though the term should say it all.

When the baker saw that it did not, he took the youngster by the arm and led him to the back of the mezzanine.

"He, like all his predecessors, allows Semites like you and me to be enslaved. Don't you know that the Hyksos would not permit this?"

Joseph had heard tales of the Hyksos, the "Shepherd Kings," a revolutionary tribe of nomads who had made inroads into the Nile economy, and who had learned to circulate capably within the society of citified Egyptians. They were a controversial people, looked on with suspicion by their Hebrew brothers and considered a threat by many of Pharaoh's advisers.

Nevertheless, their influence continued to grow, and those who advocated more humanitarian politics wished they might rise to power.

"I know something about them" Joseph replied. "Is not such talk dangerous, Phineas?"

"Dangerous, and necessary," Phineas whispered, leaning close to Joseph's ear. "I see you have much to learn."

Then, smirking again, he watched the chief butler go about his work. Tophet would not side with the Hyksos. He was a great lover of King Timaeus, proud of his pure Egyptian lineage, and a hater of Semites. Had Phineas not been such a capable servant, Tophet would not have tolerated his filling such a responsible position in the household.

But Phineas was clever and crafty. He had made a way for himself within the confines of captivity, and once regaining his independence, stayed on because it served himself best to do so.

"Tophet is far more dangerous than all the talking I might do," the baker warned. "He loves Pharaoh, and would as soon have you or me hung as allow us to breathe upon the king."

* * *

Pharaoh Timaeus would be here in two days. Anticipation was feverish in the high priest's house.

Joseph walked this afternoon with his overseer through the bazaar of On, watching carefully as Phineas bargained and haggled with the merchants.

"As a son of Israel, you are clever at market," the baker had guessed, assuming that no prince of a tribe the size of Jacob's could be less. "If you learn as quickly as I think you can, I will let you be my buyer."

Joseph knew Phineas had singled him out for this special opportunity because of their mutual heritage. He knew the baker was coming to think of him as kin, almost as a son.

"How did you happen to join Esau's tribe?" the young Hebrew asked as they wound their way between the market stalls.

"Many years ago," Phineas explained, "I was living in Edom, a Keturahite by birth."

Joseph smiled proudly. "A descendent of Abraham!" he enthused, knowing that Keturah had been Abraham's second wife. "Then we *are* brothers!"

"Thank you," Phineas said. "I should like to think so. My family and I had been hit hard by famine when I met your uncle. My elderly parents were very ill, and I, being a baker with no access to wheat, could not provide for them. It was then that I met Esau."

The man's tone was tender as he spoke the patriarch's name. Joseph recalled the fear which that word had once inspired in those of Jacob's tribe. But he had come to love Esau just as Phineas had.

"He took us in," the baker explained. "He gave us lodging and food and saved our lives. For this I devoted myself to him, and he let me be his servant."

To serve out of choice, and not compulsion, would be a fine thing, Joseph considered. Across the market square was the auction block where only weeks before he had entered into slavery.

"How did you come to be in Egypt?" the youngster inquired.

"I was abducted, just as you were," Phineas replied. "And just as thousands of our people have been, century after century. I was fortunate enough to be able to buy my freedom and become indentured. But I may as well have been a slave."

Joseph watched the ground as they walked, remembering the fields and tents of Jacob, for whom he longed with all his heart.

There was no love in Egypt, he concluded. It was a cold, unfeeling land, and hope eluded him.

Just then a disturbance at the head of the avenue drew his attention toward the temple. Descending from the acropolis, from the house of Potiphera, was a grand carriage, and the shoppers in the bazaar watched its approach with eager eyes.

Recognizing it as the carriage of the high priest's wife, they hoped to glimpse her as she rode through town. The curtains of the cab were drawn. It was unlikely that she would show her haughty face, but the chance that she might held them in worshipful suspense.

"Natira," Phineas explained. "See how these fools drool to see her!"

For Joseph, the very thought of the woman was unsettling. When a slender hand reached through the cab window, pulling one of the curtains aside, he dreaded the sight of her.

But the face which peered forth was neither haughty nor cold. It was soft and kind—the face of the young woman who had captivated him the day of Natira's banquet.

Her gaze, as she looked upon the crowd, seemed strangely compassionate, as though she saw them as individuals and not rabble.

In that instant, her eyes met Joseph's, and for a fleeting second he could have sworn she remembered him.

But just as quickly, the hand of another passenger reached over the girl's shoulder, grabbing the curtain from her light grip and closing it firmly.

"Natira," Joseph thought. "What hold do you have on my lady?"

# 25

Asenath. Her name was Asenath.

The baker had told him so. And ever since Joseph had heard the name, it had haunted him like sweet music.

He resisted its allure, believing it wrong to love an Egyptian. And he resisted the thought of her because he knew she was unattainable. She was, the baker told him, the daughter of Natira and Potiphera. Furthermore, as daughter of the high priest, she had been dedicated to the gods of Egypt from birth.

In fact, her name meant "daughter of Nath," the goddess of wisdom. Joseph thought it less than wisdom to love her.

Nevertheless, her porcelain face and winsome smile confounded him, and he knew she had been pleased to see him today when she looked out from her carriage.

Would she acknowledge him now, he wondered, were she to find him in the kitchen? He was glad that the fine ladies of the house rarely entered his workplace.

Standing in the pantry, he arranged small tins of spice and bags of yeast upon the shelves. With chagrin he thought of Jacob, grateful that his father did not witness his shame, the woman's work, the work of a slave, which was his occupation. And how he wished that Asenath might have known him in his princely role.

His face red, he gingerly touched the brand upon his neck. She could never love a slave, he knew. Yet a tribal chieftain, firstborn of Israel's favorite wife, heir to the

148

promises of Isaac—this Asenath might have found desirable.

As he went about his mundane tasks, heaviness consumed him. Where *were* the promises of Isaac? Had Joseph's dreams been nothing but mockery?

His brothers would have said so. Perhaps they were right.

Still, he knew the old shepherd of Shechem had been real, as real as the man in the cave on the night of Rachel's death.

It seemed, now, that the old fellow must have known the future, that he must have known the sorrow which lay ahead.

Downcast, Joseph turned from the pantry, overwhelmed with the misery of his existence. What worse fate could befall him, he could not imagine. For he could conceive of nothing more shameful than to live out his life as a kitchen slave to a pagan priest.

Memories of the old shepherd still filled his head as he approached the pantry arch. Beyond lay the workroom where Phineas would have yet another meaningless job for him.

But someone blocked the passageway, and the workroom was quiet and empty.

At first Joseph could scarcely believe his eyes. Natira stood in the doorway, leaning, long and slender, against the frame.

"Madam," Joseph said, bowing from the waist, "how may I serve you?"

Natira surveyed him, a catlike smile pulling at her lips.

"I shall not dine with the guests tonight," she said.

Joseph would have asked why, but he knew personal inquiries were inappropriate.

"I tire of the politics and prattle of my husband's guests," she sighed. "Timaeus arrives tomorrow and I must be rested. I shall dine in my chamber this evening. And you shall serve me."

# 26

Joseph stood at the foot of Natira's couch, his face burning. The sense of discomfort he always had in her presence was stronger tonight than ever.

Bending over, he placed a large food-laden tray upon her table, and waited while she straightened her gown and positioned herself against her pillows. "Kalat!" she snapped, calling for her chambermaid. "These cushions are stiff!"

Instantly, a young servant rushed to her mistress's aid. Gently lifting pillow after pillow from Natira's lounge, she fluffed them and replaced them carefully for her comfort.

"Enough, enough!" Natira sighed, motioning the girl away.

Every corner of the room was occupied by a servant. And there were several corners, as the room had many alcoves and arches. Most of the servants were young men, of various races, all bearing the brand upon their necks.

Joseph wondered about them, how they had come to be slaves and whether they were as uneasy in Natira's presence as he was.

When Phineas had learned that Joseph would serve the mistress this evening, he had been unusually quiet. But just as the youngster had left for the duty, the baker had taken him aside. Looking up into Joseph's face, he had whispered, "Be careful, my son."

"Phineas speaks highly of you," Natira said, as Joseph

held forth her napkin. Taking the linen, she gazed into his face and smiled.

Surprised that the subject was in context with his own thoughts, he nodded.

"I have never had a Hebrew slave," she went on. "They are a wild race, are they not? Lovers of freedom."

Across Joseph's mind flashed the desert and the mountains of Palestine, and something like anger filled his heart.

"They are, Madam," he replied.

Straightening, he eyed her with cool detachment.

"Well," she offered, "I am sure that in time you will come to like it here."

With this, she reached out a solicitous hand and stroked his wrist. "There are advantages to being my slave," she purred.

Joseph recoiled.

Silence filled the chamber as the servants looked on.

"If Madam is finished with me, Phineas needs me in the kitchen," he managed.

Natira's face reddened, and her eyes flashed.

"Certainly," she said, dismissing him with a growl. "No one needs you here."

\* \* \*

Shaking, Joseph stood in the shadows outside Natira's door. Moonlight beckoned from a balcony at the end of the hall, and seeing that no one was there, the Hebrew headed for it.

His heart drumming, he steadied himself against the balcony rail and surveyed the sprawling luxury of the acropolis. So grand a neighborhood was nowhere else on earth, but Joseph despised the streets and the walls, yearning for the wilderness of the nomads.

For a long while he stood there, taking in the music of the distant court as it wound through the mansion's twisting corridors. But he longed for the pipes and lutes of his tribal musicians and for the sight of wild-haired Israelite girls twirling and spinning in long, vivid skirts.

Joseph ran a hand over his bare head, shame coloring his face. Whenever his black hair had shown signs of growth, Tophet had seen to it that he was freshly shaven. He feared he would never again feel the comfort of curls against his neck or the warmth of his raven beard upon his cheeks.

As he brooded in solitude, the music of the court was joined by the distant laughter of women. Bracing himself, he cocked his head and listened. It seemed to be coming his way, growing louder and echoing down the hall.

Some group of females approached, and he had nowhere to run. Were he to exit through the corridor he would have to pass directly by them, and he would have to account for his presence here.

Pressing himself against the wall, he hoped the women would turn into some chamber down the way.

But he would not be so fortunate. Within moments they were entering the balcony, gathering along the rail and admiring the view.

At first no one saw Joseph. But he would not elude them for long.

"See here, what's this?" someone cried. "A man on the women's veranda!"

"Asenath, Asenath!" another called. "It is your mother's slave!"

Joseph took a sharp breath. Parting the company and standing before him was the lady of his dreams, daughter of his mistress, forbidden child of his master.

Wide-eyed, she studied him. "Leave us," she said, turning to her friends. "Let me question him."

The women, Asenath's favorite companions, obediently complied. But not without question. Shaking their heads and whispering together, they recalled the

Hebrew's insolent behavior the night of Natira's banquet, and they eyed him with suspicion.

When they had departed, Asenath tried to be firm. "You should not be here," she asserted.

"I know, my lady," Joseph managed, his throat dry.

"This place is off limits to men."

"I understand that, now," he replied. "It will not happen again."

Bowing, he backed toward the arch, ready to be sent from her presence. But she would not release him so quickly.

"How do you happen to be here?" she inquired.

Slaves were not often encouraged to explain themselves. Lifting his eyes, he found her expression warm, as it had been this afternoon in the market.

"I . . . I was summoned to serve your mother," he said.

Asenath stiffened. "I see," she replied. "And have you fulfilled your duty?"

Joseph shuffled awkwardly. "I have my lady." Asenath's face reddened, and Joseph wondered what she thought.

"I brought the mistress her meal, and I departed," he said. "I fulfilled my duty."

This seemed to relieve her. "Very well," she sighed. "Then you should return to the kitchen."

Bowing again, Joseph was about to comply, when the girl stopped him once more.

"Do you like the view from our balcony?" she asked, smiling a little.

The slave did not readily answer, and Asenath marveled. "Surely you have never seen any place more beautiful!"

"There are places more to my liking," he dared.

The girl drew back. "You? A Hebrew?" she laughed. "Whatever could you have seen to equal our city?"

Joseph took a risk in challenging her. But he cared not for his present well-being. Mountains and hills called him, and he would as soon die as be removed forever from them.

"I have seen places without walls," he answered, "places where the wind is the very breath of God. I have heard the desert sing and have possessed the stars at night. My Lady, you should be so wealthy as to own what I have owned."

# 27

Joseph waited along the back wall of On's most sacred chamber, the inner sanctum of the Temple of Ra. He, as well as all the other slaves of Potiphera's house, must be present at the reception of Pharaoh, which would take place here within moments.

Every year, Phineas had explained, King Timaeus came to this room, directly upon arriving in On. Here he would receive the blessing of the high priest and be ordained for yet another twelve months as ruler of the realm.

Of all the shames heaped upon the son of Jacob, this experience brought him lowest. For one who carried Jehovah in his heart, to witness the rites of pagan worship was unthinkable.

The stone walls of the chamber were cold to his back. His bare head, likewise, was cold, and he rubbed his hands together behind him.

Tall temple slaves with long slender beards, the only slaves allowed to go unshaven, stepped through the door at the back of the hall. In their hands they carried elegant tapers, the tips flickering with flame. Toward the platform at the front of the room they marched, followed close by beardless eunuchs in white robes. These eunuchs pounded small hand drums and rattled tambourines in cadence with the candlebearers' step.

Earlier in the day a grand parade, replete with flashing chariots, stamping stallions, and dancing girls, had brought Pharaoh into town. This evening's processional was shorter and simpler, in keeping with its hallowed purpose. On the heels of the eunuchs were more slaves, these bearing trumpets and heralding the entrance of the king.

When Joseph saw Timaeus, a chill passed through him. A giant of a man, his stature suited his position as emperor of the world. A broad, striped headdress fell to broader shoulders, and the sun-disk glistened on his bare torso.

His face, cold as iron, revealed a merciless heart, and he had apparently well-earned his reputation as a ruthless, unrelenting ruler.

Ceremoniously he walked toward the platform, flanked on each side by attendants. Normally Pharaoh would have been carried on slaves' shoulders, in a handsome cab borne atop horizontal poles. But in the Temple of Ra, he walked like any commoner.

The king looked straight ahead, not allowing his eyes to wander from the altar at the center of the platform. As he approached, Potiphera emerged from a curtained alcove.

Rarely since coming to dwell here had Joseph seen Potiphera. As he observed him now, he saw the same quiet dignity, the same kindness that had reached out to save him in the marketplace.

The ordination ceremony would be brief. To the rhythm of the soft drums, Pharaoh bowed before his priest. And the slaves with the long candles lit a fire upon the altar.

Holding forth a golden chalice, Potiphera poured the blood of some freshly slain beast through the flames, and it sent an acrid smoke toward the ceiling.

Countless times Joseph had watched as his own father performed a similar rite on the wilderness altars of his tribe. But as he had done so, he had sung hymns to Jehovah. Today, Potiphera invoked the blessings of Ra upon the king, chanting a theogony in ancient Egyptian.

Though Joseph could not understand the words, he was repelled by them.

He might have witnessed all this with less resentment, however, had Asenath not entered on the scene.

Apparently taking a cue from her father's words, she emerged from the same alcove and joined the priest on stage.

Speaking now in common Egyptian, the priest introduced her as the goddess of wisdom, "daughter of Nath," and holder of the secrets of life.

The young Hebrew was appalled at her appearance. Though she was still lovely and innocent of face, she was garbed in gaudy gold from head to toe, and her fluid gown was embellished with pagan emblems. Her eyes, painted darker than usual, held fast to the king, and as she stepped forth, she placed her hands upon his head.

Wisdom was to be the hallmark of a Pharaoh—for Pharaoh was the god of light incarnate.

Thus, in symbolic ceremony, he and the goddess were joined, light and wisdom energizing one another.

The ritual complete, Timaeus was asked to stand, and the procession led him forth to a new year of power.

As Joseph watched the king pass by, he wondered how he—an enslaver of men, a worshiper of false gods—could be considered wise.

And he wondered if gentle Asenath were beyond redemption.

# 28

Pharaoh and his entourage had been vacationing at Potiphera's mansion for two months. With their stay, Joseph's responsibilities had expanded.

Phineas's assessment of Joseph's abilities, his assumption that as prince of a Hebrew tribe the youngster was highly capable, was not unfounded. And though Tophet, the chief butler, had resisted his swift advancement, even he had come to admit that Joseph was an asset to the workroom.

Gradually Joseph was called upon to oversee the tasks of slaves and servants who had worked for Potiphera for years. Already he served as the baker's chief buyer, as first assistant at all banquets, and as manager of Tophet's waiters.

One of the privileges of the Hebrew's increased authority was that it brought him into more frequent contact with Potiphera. Although he had been purchased for Natira, he was, from time to time, called upon to run personal errands for the high priest or to make purchases directly related to his chamber. As their daily interaction developed, he sensed that the high priest enjoyed his company.

This evening he accompanied Tophet to serve at a select gathering of Pharaoh's officials. Often, when Timaeus was present in On, the chief butler served as royal cupbearer, and he must focus full attention on the task of keeping the king's cup filled. Therefore, he must pass his regular duties as governor of the dinner to another. It was Joseph who would fill that capacity this day.

Although servants and slaves were supposed to be deaf to the conversations of their masters during such engagements, the gossip of the court always fell readily on their ears. Tonight Pharaoh and Potiphera, along with all their aides, discussed economic matters, and Joseph listened with ardent interest as he oversaw the smooth running of the meal.

It seemed a minor famine in Goshen had produced a setback in the wheat crop, and Pharaoh and those around him collaborated on the matter of making up for the dearth with imports.

They could not agree upon where to find the cheapest prices. And Joseph itched to share an opinion.

They considered Gilead, where gentle rains and winds produced the finest crops. But the cost of Gilead wheat could be prohibitive. They wondered about Phoenicia, but while the seafoods from that land were excellent, the farm produce was never of the highest quality.

At last Joseph could restrain himself no longer.

"Shechem," he muttered.

Potiphera, attuned to Joseph's voice, asked him to speak up.

"Shechem wheat will be fine this spring," Joseph offered.

"Do tell," the priest marveled. "How do you know this?"

The advisers whispered around the table, wondering at the slave's boldness and at Potiphera's indulgence.

"Winter was hard in the Vale of Shalem last year," he explained, recalling his days of miserable wandering in quest of his brothers. "The seeds that manage to survive in the ground will come up hardy and rich in that part of Palestine."

Timaeus leaned over, conferring with Potiphera, and as he did, one of his advisers smirked. "Palestine was hit hard from border to border that season. What is so special about Shechem?"

Joseph did not remind them that the little city had been burned to the ground a few years before. Nor would he reveal the part his own family had played in that devastation.

"The economy of the vale is very poor." he simply said. "The locals would settle for a bargain price."

The counselors looked at one another in amazement, but the first challenger was still not convinced.

"The lad is Hebrew," Potiphera reminded them. "He speaks of things he knows."

"Very well, sir," the adviser conceded. "Then perhaps the Hebrew can shed light on the matter of the wool we imported last year. Did it not come from heather-fed sheep along his country's coast? It was some of the poorest we have received."

"Do not go to the coast for your wool," Joseph responded. "You will receive a good price, but only because the seacoast is not shepherd country. Rather, go east, even east of my people. The region of Zoar has ash in the soil, and the grass is as lush as a Lebanon forest. The sheep there grow fat and their coats are like blankets. You will pay more, but you will not regret it."

The men were dumbfounded, never having considered the plain where Sodom and Gomorrah once stood to be worth much of anything.

"Also, sirs," Joseph went on, his voice picking up courage, "you will find a treasure in the sands of that region. Dig down and there are carpets of green glass, glass superior to anything the Phoenicians produce, hidden to all but the bedouins who know the source."

Pharaoh was quizzical. "Indeed," he laughed. "And what is the source?"

"The God of my people destroyed the cities of the plain years ago," the youngster said matter-of-factly. "He destroyed them with brimstone, which accounts for the ash in the ground. And he destroyed them with unearthly fire, which melted the very sands of the wilderness."

At this, the company hooted. "Just who is this god of whom you speak?" Timaeus sneered, pressing him like an offended deity.

"My God is the God of the desert and the sea, the winds and the cities. He is God over all the earth, though its people do not remember him."

Potiphera, stunned by the lad's daring, gripped the arms of his chair. When Pharaoh started angrily, he reached out a hand to console him.

"Let the lad speak," he counseled. "Surely Your Majesty is not troubled by the ravings of a shepherd boy."

The king, confounded, kept a seething silence. But the ministers were not appeased.

Jeering, they challenged him again. "What other advice does this upstart have?" they mocked. "Perhaps he can save the land of Egypt!"

Joseph knew they referred to more than economics. Had he been careless of his life, he would have counseled them, then and there, to evict their emperor and bring in the Hyksos.

"If you are purchasing your horses from the Midianites, you could do better," he suggested, trying to be respectful.

Again, they laughed. "We have *always* purchased our mounts from the Arabs! The whole world knows they are the finest stock on earth!"

"Not so fine as the horses of the Edomites," Joseph offered, remembering Esau's beautiful herds. "The horses of Jordan are bred on wind and wild wheat. They are restive, but tamable. And when they obey the rein, they are the gentlest creatures under heaven."

A hush filled the chamber as the young Hebrew shared his knowledge on yet other topics.

Tophet, who stood at Pharaoh's elbow, was incredulous.

What manner of fellow was this who had come to serve in his kitchen? He feared, now, for his own position. And with good reason.

In time, should the youngster's advice prove worthy, he could take over management of the entire house.

# PART IV
# The Accused

# 29

Potiphera walked with Joseph through the grain fields beyond the wall of On. The property, which belonged to the high priest, had not yielded as well as he wished for several years, and he watched today with his Hebrew slave as his farmers tilled ash into the soil.

This practice was new to the priest, and he tried it as an experiment at Joseph's suggestion.

Potiphera's face glowed with anticipation as he dreamed of the crops he might harvest in the fall.

Joseph had served Potiphera four years, working for him now as much as for Natira. Every idea he had shared with Potiphera and his advisers had borne fruit. The purchase of Shechem wheat had been a boon to Egypt's economy and had seen it through a hard year. The wool of Zoar was exceptionally fine, just as the Hebrew had said. And Pharaoh had begun to outfit his stables with the horses of Edom.

This last suggestion Joseph had made with secret motive, knowing that as Esau prospered, so would his brother Jacob. For the two tribes were interdependent, and what good befell one was sure to bear on the good of the other.

Joseph had never told Potiphera about his family. He still spoke of himself as a Hebrew, with no reference to his tribe. And respecting his privacy, his master had never pressed him.

As they passed this day through the grain fields, Potiphera placed an arm about Joseph's shoulders. "You have been a blessing to me," the priest said. "Have I ever told you so?"

"Many times, sir," Joseph replied with a smile.

For a quiet moment, Potiphera was deep in thought. "Almost would I think you the son I never had," he confessed. "It seems everything I place in your hand prospers."

Joseph was flattered, but his heart was pricked with memories of his true father, Jacob, and of the sonship he had with him.

"It is truly amazing how successful you are," Potiphera continued. "Sometimes I believe this god of yours must be as great as the Sun."

The Hebrew knew the priest was being facetious, but he took his comment seriously.

"With all respect, sir, my God is greater. He made the sun and all the stars."

With this, Joseph privately recalled the vision he had had the night of his bar mitzvah, the waking dream of the humbled stars, the bowing sun and moon. Longing and sadness, which he had managed to suppress with his busy schedule, rose up from a dark place within.

But his master did not read his feelings.

"I should be angry with you when you speak so," Potiphera sighed. "But so long as your beliefs do not interfere with your work, I cannot be."

Such was the liberality of the Egyptian religious system, a system which accepted all worship and had, in fact, made all creatures sacred. Joseph might have admired the priest's indulgence, but knew it was based on a loose theology.

"What I really wish to address is your future with me," the master explained. "Do you see all this?" he said, gesturing to the fields which stretched for miles in every direction. "All of this I place within your keeping, along with my whole house. As of this day, you shall be my chief steward, overseeing all my affairs so that I may devote myself to study and contemplation, which is my rightful duty. No one shall be over you in my house, and everyone who serves me shall serve you. Are you pleased?"

Was he pleased? Joseph stared at Potiphera as though he were not real, as though the words he had just spoken could not be part of any language.

"Master!" he marveled. "How can this be? I am but a slave, a thing of purchase..."

"Stop, Joseph!" Potiphera commanded. "Never speak so of yourself. From this day, you are no longer my slave, but my chief overseer."

They had come to the highway which ran through the fields. Potiphera's carriage awaited them, and taking their seats inside, they headed for the acropolis.

The young Hebrew's head still spun with the announcement as they approached the gate of Potiphera's mansion.

"See here?" the priest added, indicating the gracious residence and its many outbuildings. "All of this is in your hands. Nothing you ask shall be withheld from you."

Suddenly, however, the man's eyes were caught away to the sight of his wife, who was sitting upon her balcony high above. Her hairdresser brushed her dark hair in the afternoon sun, making it shine like polished onyx.

"Nothing shall be withheld from you," he repeated, "save Natira."

Joseph could scarcely believe his ears. That the master could even consider the possibility of such betrayal was appalling.

But the Hebrew said nothing, noting the man's love-struck gaze as he observed the mistress.

"She is my life, Joseph," he whispered. "My very life."

# 30

Nearly seven more years had passed in gratifying peace as Joseph fulfilled his service to Potiphera. The high priest's prosperity doubled under the Hebrew's administration, and everyone came to view Joseph as chief overseer of the house.

Even Tophet bowed to the Hebrew, although his resentments were never mollified.

Early on Potiphera had encouraged Joseph to let his hair and beard grow. "Wear them in the manner of an Egyptian," he suggested, "but do not shave them again."

In robes of wealth was Joseph attired, his luxurious beard crimped stylishly and his dark locks loosely fettered by laces of pure gold. His garments, though never as much to his liking as the long-lost coat which his father had given him, were of the finest linen, edged in lavender, his master's color.

Tonight a sweet breeze off the river of On wafted through the mansion's rooftop garden. Joseph never ceased to remember the wilderness of Israel and the freedom of his nomad existence. But he always found a measure of solace in the quiet bowers of this place.

Across the parapet that enclosed the roof was a magnificent view to the north, and often in private meditation the Hebrew would study the distant desert, dreaming of the day when he might return to his father's people.

He was a free man now, not a slave. He could demand

his right to leave the country. But he had come to love Potiphera and to believe his service here was of value.

Furthermore, he sensed that the timing was not right for his departure, that if his God planned for him to go home, it was not to be just yet.

His father surely thought him long dead. His brothers likely wished to believe so themselves, and had never told Jacob of their cruelty toward him.

Whatever the case with his family, every time he thought to return, something restrained him.

Tonight, the week before his seventh anniversary as Potiphera's steward, he contemplated upcoming events. The high priest had planned a great banquet in his honor and had told him to consider his future well. For he would be giving him a reward, and Joseph must be prepared to ask whatever he wished of his master.

Years ago, when the priest had first told him of his new position, he had said he would withhold nothing from Joseph. All that he had was at the Hebrew's disposal, save Natira.

There really was nothing he lacked, Joseph thought as he pondered the offer, nothing but the fellowship of close kin. He knew not what to request and was concerned lest he disappoint his generous lord.

As Joseph studied the sunset desert, a light footfall roused him from his thoughts. Turning about, he saw that Asenath had entered the garden. After all these years, the sight of her still never failed to stir his heart.

Always he had steeled himself against his feelings for the young lady. Yet as he had become an intimate part of the priest's household, he had found himself falling more and more in love with her.

Though they were rarely alone, their few private conversations were always rich with wonder and sharing.

Asenath was no longer a girl. Tonight, more than ever, Joseph could see this. Tall and willowy, she had reached full-flowered womanhood, her arms soft and supple beneath her shawl, her breasts high and round beneath her clinging gown. Yet never had she married, unwilling to settle for any of her many courtiers.

However, her face always seemed to light when she saw Joseph, and her voice was laced with music.

Such was the case just now as she discovered his vigil in the garden.

"Joseph," she called, hurrying toward him through the twilight. "I thought I might find you here."

Joining him at the railing, she laughed gaily. "Father says there will be a dinner in your honor next week. How proud you must be!"

The Hebrew smiled down upon her. "Your father is very kind."

"It is not kindness!" Asenath objected. "It is duty. No one deserves recognition more than you. Father would be remiss to overlook your loyal service."

Bowing, Joseph conceded. "Never has he overlooked me, my lady. But I am pleased that you are pleased."

Asenath quietly followed his gaze as he turned again to the rail. The northern folds of wilderness, as it stretched toward the great unseen sea, were purple and gold.

"Father will have you say a few words that evening, to all the company. Will you speak of your God?"

Surprised at the introduction of this topic, Joseph considered the idea. "If it is appropriate," he said. "Why do you ask?"

"You speak of him often. Many here would like to know more about him."

Joseph read a peculiar longing in her tone, a longing that had manifested itself many times.

"Are you among them?" he asked, trying not to show his eager hope.

"I was taught by my father to represent wisdom," she said. Nervously she ran a slender finger along the marble balustrade. "I have studied beside him in the libraries of

On, and I was raised on prayers to the goddess of understanding."

Joseph listened with respect. "There is much to know about divine things," he agreed. "But there is no god or goddess who can teach you. Only the One True God, the Maker of all, is capable of that."

Asenath could have been offended. But to his amazement, she was not. Gently she touched his sleeve, sending a charge of sweet energy through him.

"What is the name of this God?" she inquired. "You have never told me."

Joseph sighed, shaking his head. "I do not know," he confessed. "We call him 'Jehovah,' 'the Lord.' But to my knowledge, there is no man or woman on earth who has heard his name."

He knew this seemed very strange and might make his testimony implausible.

"I only know that my father, grandfather and great-grandfather—and I myself—have encountered him," he went on. "He is a mover of the heart. And he is moving yours just now. Is he not, Asenath?"

The woman was captivated by his witness. Unable to deny her longings, she nodded.

Bending over her, Joseph steadfastly studied her face. He knew now what he would ask of his master, what his request would be.

This woman was a kindred spirit, and he longed to make her his own.

With a daring borne of unfettered love, he caressed her bare shoulder, and she, yielding, entered his embrace.

For the first time in Joseph's life, he felt the ache of passion, and pressing his lips to hers, he dreamed of its fulfillment.

# 31

There was only one drawback to the Hebrew's privileged station in the house of Potiphera. His elevated position brought him into daily contact with Natira.

Though she had not touched him since the long-ago evening when she had called him to serve dinner in her chamber, her attraction to him had never been veiled. Often she had let him know, by innuendo and direct statement, that she desired his company.

Generally, however, Joseph's spirits were high as he went about his work.

Especially this day was his heart merry, as he anticipated the banquet and his planned request for Asenath's hand in marriage. The kiss they had shared the evening before told him the lady was willing, but he must first secure the approval of her father.

When Phineas knocked on the door of his office, where Joseph was tabulating stacks of accounting tablets, the baker's crestfallen face clashed with the Hebrew's joyful mood.

"What is it, friend?" he asked. "This is too grand a day for unhappiness."

"Indeed, it should be, Master," Phineas agreed, calling him by his rightful title. "I hope my news means no trouble for you."

"What could trouble me today?" he laughed. "It is a bright future which spreads before us. Yes, Phineas, I plan not only to ask my own reward at the banquet, but to request honors for you and Tophet as well."

"You are too kind," the baker said, bowing. But his brow was still furrowed. "It seems that Potiphera is not the only one dispensing awards. Our lady, Natira, requests your company in her chamber, that she may . . . honor you, as well."

Joseph rolled his eyes, something he would have done in no one else's presence. "Well," he sighed, placing the accounting tablets in a neat pile, "what is the worst that can happen? It is only an inconvenience."

Phineas tried to agree. "Of course, sir," he said through a strained smile. "But do be careful."

\* \* \*

Joseph had never grown accustomed to seeing Natira reclined upon her couch. She was gifted at it, like a lounging snake upon a limb.

He had learned how to handle her advances, her seductive smiles and suggestive comments. As long as she did not touch him, he could work around her, ignoring her beguiling devices and deflecting her attempts with kind detachment.

Today, however, Natira was at her best, her vampish skills finely honed, her beauty most insistent. And when he entered her room, he cringed. For they were alone.

Not one slave, valet, or chambermaid occupied her chamber. Every station was vacant where an attendant usually stood. Every alcove was silent.

Perhaps Natira presumed that since the subtler approach had never worked, straightforward eagerness would. Her intentions had never been so blatant.

"Sit with me," she hissed, moving over on her bed and patting the mattress. "You are an honored servant. Let me reward you."

Joseph's cheeks colored. "Surely Madam has some service . . . something I may do for her . . ." he stammered.

This only evoked a gleaming smile and Joseph reconsidered.

"May I fetch something..." he choked.

"You fear Potiphera," she cooed. "The master is away. He will not be back until evening. Here," she beckoned, pulling her legs toward the back of the couch, "lie with me."

Joseph's face burned. But he maintained his dignity.

"Madam," he argued, "Potiphera is my friend as well as my master. With me in charge, my master does not concern himself with anything in the house, and he has put all that he owns in my hands. There is no one greater in this house than I, and he has withheld nothing from me except you, because you are his wife. How then could I do this great evil and sin against God?"

With this, he clenched his fists and headed for the door. His heart pounding, he hastened toward the safety of the busy household.

Never would he tell a soul of Natira's plot. And never again would he go near her chamber alone.

# 32

Only two days remained before the banquet. Although the event was in honor of Joseph, it required much extra work on his part.

As overseer of the house, preparation for any such affair demanded his attention.

Since morning, he had been in every corner of the mansion, seeing to it that the chambermaids had made up the guest rooms and that all things were in order for the meal and the entertainment.

Though Pharaoh was not due for his annual vacation in On, he would be coming early from Memphis for the feast. His arrival alone had required days of planning.

All this busy work helped to take Joseph's mind off the encounter with Natira. And it helped him avoid being near her.

The few times they passed in the hallway or were obliged to consult together, he was in company, and she must settle for giving him cutting looks instead of words.

He hoped there would be no further incident before the banquet. Once Potiphera promised Asenath's hand in marriage, Natira would surely keep her distance.

The day was exceptionally hot for early spring. Joseph had just seen to the unloading of supplies in the gate outside and hastened now to other work in the main portion of the house.

Potiphera and his officials were in a cabinet meeting this afternoon. The baker and butler were with the women servants in the kitchen wing, and the menservants were working in the fields.

The house was very quiet, a relief to Joseph's overtaxed mind. As he passed down the empty corridor leading toward his office, he halted at the sound of his name.

It was more a lisp than a real word—more an evocative challenge than a name.

Wheeling about, he saw the woman in the shadows, her chest rising and falling as though her pulse pounded madly.

Against her breast she held a long-legged cat, one of the family pets, and she stroked its dense ebony fur as though she were herself feline.

"Joseph," she purred again.

Natira was fingering the slack at the neck of her gown. Gently she lowered the cat to the floor and pulled the silky fabric of her dress downward, revealing the cleft of her bosom.

Dumbfounded, Joseph tried to inch past her so he might head back outside.

Then he felt it. Her touch. Her grasping hands upon his garment.

"Lie with me!" she commanded.

"Lord Jehovah!" he cried, tearing free and rushing blindly for the door.

In Natira's clutches he left his cloak, ripped from his shoulders as he fled.

And as he hastened outside, he heard her cries, her hateful revenge.

"Rape! Rape!" shrieked the scorned Natira. "Oh, help me! Guards!"

# 33

In a swoon-like sleep Joseph dreamed he was in the wilderness cistern, cast off by his brothers and left to die. No sun pounded down upon him, but life seeped from him like the sweat of a fever.

In his torment, his dreaming eyes scanned the cistern's lip, longing to see the old shepherd. The sight of him might inspire hope, but he was nowhere to be found.

Across the desert, the sound of caravans approached, and he relived the fear of capture. Jolting awake, he found that the rumbling was not of wagon wheels, but the tramping of feet, guards outside his prison cell.

Straightening his cramped body, he leaned against the mossy wall of Potiphera's dungeon, and he winced at the pain in his shackled ankles.

As the guards passed his door, he called out to them. "Send for Master Potiphera!" he cried. "Surely he will hear my defense. Send for Phineas. He will vouch for my character!"

But no one heeded his plea. "So the chief Hebrew has come to this!" the guards mocked, reveling in his overthrow. "You would be better off a sandflea once again!"

Voluptuous Natira filled Joseph's head, her steamy smile and slick accusation stripping him of hope. He knew she must have spun a convincing lie, one which could lock him away forever.

He could imagine it now. She would have waved his cloak like a banner. "See here," she must have said, "he left his garment in my hand as he fled. Is this not proof that he tried to take me? Is it not proof that I struggled against him?"

And he could imagine his dear master, disillusioned, heartsick, filled with wrath at the supposed betrayal.

Huddling against the cold floor, he fought tears. Tomorrow there would be a banquet in the mansion, the banquet which should have been his own. With Pharaoh and a host of guests due to arrive, it was too late for the affair to be canceled.

And so Potiphera would find other reasons to make merry. Light and laughter would fill the dining hall while Joseph sat in lonely darkness, the vacuum of despair his only cellmate.

The Hebrew would be asked after. Guests would wonder why he was not there, and when they heard Natira's tale, they would hate him as though eleven years of faithful service were not evidence of his character.

Better would it be to die, he believed, than to dwell in this netherland of outcasts. Better would it be if he had never been taught that Jehovah cared.

For faith had departed, and perpetual night was Joseph's lot.

\* \* \*

When the evening of Joseph's feast arrived, Tophet fretfully bustled about the kitchen, trying to do two jobs at once.

He was, as usual, governor of the dining hall. But tonight he was also filling Phineas's shoes, managing the mundane tasks of the workroom.

Exasperated, he glanced toward a corner of the pantry. Phineas was slumped upon a chair, a wine bottle in his hand.

When Tophet had found him in this drunken state, it had been time to prepare the main course. Propping him in the storeroom, he had left him there and told the servants to start cooking without him.

Now, however, Phineas was becoming rowdy, calling attention to himself with loud talk.

"We must keep him quiet!" the butler growled, grabbing the bottle from his hand. "Brew up the strongest tea you can find!"

As guests began to file into the dining room, servant after servant attempted to force the potent liquid down the baker's throat. But all efforts to sober him up were of no avail.

Tophet should have resigned any hope of having his coworker's help tonight. He should have sent him to his room as soon as he began to rave.

For Phineas was beyond self-pity, beyond quiet slobber. He was beyond calling out for Joseph and blaming himself for not warning him more strongly.

Phineas was becoming belligerent, his slurred words growing in volume. As they reached past the kitchen walls, they put Tophet and his entire crew in danger.

"Potiphera is a fool!" he ranted. "Natira is a whore! Pharaoh is a king of whores and fools!"

Suddenly the merrymaking in the banquet hall tapered to shocked silence. Potiphera rose up on his dinner couch, clutching at his napkin. Darting a startled glance at Pharaoh, he saw that his own neck was at stake and instantly sent to see who was responsible for the insults.

When word returned that the baker was drunk, Potiphera called for his dismissal. As guards were sent for Phineas, his raving continued to spill forth from the workroom.

"Tophet is the baker's overseer, is he not?" Timaeus recalled, his face livid.

"He is," Potiphera stammered.

"They must *both* be dismissed!" the king shouted. "Both of them to the darkest cell of your prison!"

# 34

A flash of torchlight filled Joseph's cell, waking him from fitful slumber. The scuffle of feet and the creaking of hinges told him someone was being thrust through the door.

The light revealed several men, two guards and two captives. As the Hebrew's eyes adjusted, he recognized Tophet and Phineas.

Scrambling to his feet, he watched in amazement as the door was slammed in the butler's face. Tophet clung to the bars of the door's small window, shouting epithets at the departing guards, and Phineas hung his wine-soaked head in bewildered horror.

"You can't do this!" Tophet yelled. "I have always been loyal to Pharaoh! The most loyal servant in the house!"

He was answered by the sound of fading footsteps.

What little light filtered through the doorgrate revealed Joseph in the corner, and when Tophet wheeled about, finding him there, he snarled like a dog.

"This is what comes of giving a Hebrew authority!" he swore. "I never trusted you from the day you came here! Seducing our lady! Upsetting the entire house! It is a wonder Pharaoh did not have our necks!"

Of course, Joseph knew nothing of what had led to their incarceration. Seeking an explanation, he turned to Phineas, who still held his head and moaned.

"Have some respect, Tophet!" the baker managed. "You know Joseph is innocent!"

"And what of *you*? the butler growled. "It was your traitorous ranting that brought this fate upon us! You have always wanted Timaeus overthrown, haven't you! I almost suspect you would side with the Hyksos, given a chance!"

"Oh . . ." Phineas groaned, rubbing his throbbing temples. "Joseph, come to me. Let me see you."

"So, I have brought you with me, old friend," Joseph sighed, dragging his ankle chain and creeping toward him. Receiving his embrace, he gently chastised him. "You are too loyal to me, Phineas. See where it has gotten you."

But Phineas paid him no mind. "See here, Tophet! Chains upon our master's feet! Is there any doubt that he suffers unjustly? You know how Natira is!"

"Hush!" Tophet commanded. "Would you have us die?"

"Then you admit it! You know Natira is a . . ."

"Enough!" Tophet cried. "I know no such thing."

"Everyone knows it!" Phineas insisted. "Even Potiphera knows it in his heart!"

"There is *nothing* to know!" the butler choked. "Quiet, or you'll have us dead!"

"Aha! See, Joseph. He admits it. Why, there is no one in the house or in the entire city who wonders why Natira fills her chamber with young men. No one . . ."

At this, Tophet leapt across the room, grappling Phineas to the floor and throttling him.

Despite his restraints, Joseph managed to intervene and, holding the men apart, shouted, "Indeed you will both die if you are not careful. You will kill *one another*!"

The two wrestlers took heed, and as silence descended, each went to his corner.

Joseph, shaking his head, found his own cold station and closed his eyes, wondering at the insanity of his world.

\* \* \*

The high priest's prison was not a quiet place. In the two weeks he had been held here, Joseph had become accustomed to the constant comings and goings of the place.

As high priest, Potiphera was also "captain of the royal bodyguard." This was not a military title, but a diplomatic and religious one, meaning that as minister of the sun god it followed that he was responsible for Pharaoh's welfare. Since Pharaoh was believed to be Ra in the flesh, the incarnate revelation of the divine, Potiphera was in charge of protecting him from danger.

Joseph's supposed crime was against the high priest's house, and Tophet and Phineas were considered political prisoners. Apparently the dungeons were full of such unfortunates, many accused as unjustly as these three.

Rarely did Potiphera set foot in the prison. Joseph had asked to see him many times, wishing to give his version of what had happened in Natira's room. But he knew the high priest would never receive his testimony, being blindly devoted to his vampish wife.

Day and night there was traffic outside Joseph's cell.

Pharaoh was a fickle tyrant, judging with little reference to evidence. Men and women could be locked away on the most trivial witness, or could be released on his whim.

Therefore, when Joseph heard the approaching tramp of guards, he paid it no mind. When it stopped before his door, however, and when he heard a woman's voice, he sat up and listened.

A torch was held close to the door grate, near enough to reveal the identity of a visitor, and the Hebrew's breath came sharply.

Asenath's pensive face peered through the opening, and urgently she called his name. Crossing the room, he grasped the bars, Tophet and Phineas close behind.

"My lady," Joseph cried, "what brings you to this awful place?"

"I implored my father to let me come," she said, "to deliver this to you."

Through the bars she passed a sealed letter, its parchment fine as linen. "It was the best he could bring himself to do," she added, as Joseph hastily opened the paper.

Reading the contents, his eyes widened. "What is this?" he gasped. "Potiphera is placing me in charge of the prison!"

"There is trouble in the streets," Asenath explained. "Threats of a Hyksos revolution. Father will need all the help he can get to manage this place."

Phineas clutched at Joseph's cloak. "Hyksos!" he whispered.

"In other words, Timaeus will institute a purge," Joseph guessed, his brow furrowed. "The prison will be more crowded than ever."

"It was the best my father could do," Asenath repeated.

When Joseph looked at her quizzically, she added, "The best he could do to make restitution."

"Restitution?" Joseph enthused. "Then he believes me!"

"Father was very angry," Asenath went on, "but he knows in his heart..."

She could not bring herself to accuse her mother aloud, but Phineas nudged Tophet triumphantly.

"Oh, Joseph," she asserted, "Father has not been himself since he sent you here. He has not slept or eaten. But when he learned that mother had blamed him for her 'shame,' he began to see that he had done you wrong."

"How could Natira blame Potiphera?" the Hebrew marveled.

"She told everyone that he had purposely brought you into our home to make fools of us, to make sport of her. This he could not abide, and now for the first time Father questions my mother's... goodwill. Perhaps," she apologized, "if Father were not so proud... if he would not lose

Natira forever, he would clear your name entirely and set you free."

Joseph sighed and shook his head. "Do not fret," he said. "God is with me." Then hesitating, "But the prison will be full of Semites, people of the desert... my own kind! How can I be their master?"

Phineas, for the first time openly declaring himself, stepped in front of the Hebrew.

"Consider yourself their comforter," he said. "As keeper of the prison, you will have power to ease their lot."

# 35

Such a colorful lot of Semites as came to occupy Joseph's prison and his time, he had never before encountered.

The revolutionaries who were incarcerated during Pharaoh's purge were of many tribes and nations. They came with countless dialects and clothing styles, and Joseph, as manager of the dungeon, allowed them to be housed according to their backgrounds.

While such people were typically earthy and freedom loving, these folk were the most outspoken of their kind. Constantly they plotted and schemed escape. And while in his heart he supported their cause, Joseph would have found it hard to love them if they had not been Hebrews.

Surly and profane, they drove him to distraction. They had heard of Joseph and of the fate which had befallen him at Natira's hands. They sympathized with his plight, but could not forgive his attachment to Potiphera.

It mattered nothing to them that he told them the priest had once saved his life. They could imagine no good in an Egyptian official.

The only reasoning which seemed to reach through their prejudice was Joseph's belief that God had brought him here, and that the full reason for his captivity in Egypt had not yet been revealed.

Joseph did not make the mistake of telling them of his youthful visions. He had learned to never again broadcast the prophecies which had sustained him all these years.

Nor did he yield to the temptation to ask after news of his father or his brothers, who were doubtless well-known in the widest of Hebrew circles. For his family's sake, he continued to keep his identity a secret. But he reveled in the Hebrews' common faith in the One God, a strain of belief which ran through their heritage, passed down from many patriarchs.

It was his unspeakable sorrow to witness Pharaoh's brutalities against his friends. Nearly every day he must stand by as men and women were led forth to execution.

So far, Tophet and Phineas had been spared, most likely because Timaeus had forgotten their minor case. But if Phineas continued to proclaim his kinship with the Hebrews, he might be taken yet.

It was early morning. Joseph had just left the guard house, where Potiphera had provided him a modest apartment, and he felt the winter sun upon his face.

All night he had been awake, his stomach knotted and his nerves frayed as group after group of captives was led forth to slaughter.

Pharaoh was on a rampage, and Joseph was helpless against it.

Bowing his head, he hastened through the prison yard on his way to the dungeon. Above, suspended from high gallows, were the swaying bodies of the dead. Mouths agape, the corpses stared at him, accusing, mocking, as all about them black crows circled, pecking at their flesh.

Time after time Joseph had wondered if he were a traitor to his kind, a coward for not throwing himself in with them and meeting the executioner's noose. But whenever he thought to do so, something caught him, some word or impression, telling him that the prophecies must be fulfilled and that his calling lay further down the road.

And so his fellow Semites sometimes hated him just as the Egyptians had hated him, just as his own brothers had. And sometimes he hated himself.

His feet leaden, he walked down the dungeon corridor, ready to check up on his remaining prisoners. As he came near the hold of Tophet and Phineas, he heard low talking within, as deathly and somber as the ache in his own heart.

Working the key in the lock, he called out to them, and entering, found them more downcast than usual, huddled together upon their blanket pile.

"What is it, friends?" he asked. "Why are your faces so sad today?"

Phineas shook his head. "We have each had dreams this night, and they are very mysterious. So clear and yet so puzzling. We have no one to tell us what they could mean."

Tophet nodded, his brow crinkled.

"The interpretation of dreams belongs to God," Joseph said, suddenly intrigued. "Tell me, please, what you dreamed."

Tophet looked askance at the Hebrew, wondering why he should share his experience with an enemy. But at last he shrugged.

"In my dream, there was a vine in front of me, and on the vine were three branches," he said. "As it was budding, its blossoms came out, and it produced ripe grapes. Now Pharaoh's cup was in my hand, so I took the grapes and squeezed them into his cup, and put it into the king's hand."

Joseph was quiet for a long while, until Tophet laughed.

"See, Phineas. What does this man know?" he mocked.

But Joseph leaned forward. "This is the interpretation," he declared. "Within three more days Pharaoh will lift up your head and restore you to your office. And you will put his cup into his hand, just as you used to do when you were his cupbearer!"

A smile lit the Hebrew's face as he shared this, and the two prisoners studied him in amazement, impressed almost as much by his authoritative confidence as by what he had said.

"Just keep me in mind when it goes well with you, friend," Joseph added. "Do me the kindness of mentioning me to Pharaoh, and get me out of this place."

Tophet, still speechless, only stared at him. And now Joseph was pressing him, his hand upon his knee.

"I was kidnapped out of my own country," he asserted. "I was sold into bondage and then falsely accused before Pharaoh. Please remember me."

Tophet sat back against the wall. "First let's see what becomes of your prophecy," he muttered.

But Phineas was greatly moved. "Sir," he begged, "hear my dream as well. Perhaps it is equally happy. If I am freed, you know I would never forget you!"

"Of course," Joseph agreed.

"In my dream I carried three baskets of white bread on my head. In the top basket there were all sorts of baked goods for Pharaoh, and the birds were eating them out of the basket."

The baker's eyes were round, as he anxiously awaited the good news.

But Joseph was silent longer this time, until Phineas grew apprehensive.

"Sir..." he whispered. "Don't toy with me. Tell me I shall go free..."

The younger Hebrew choked back tears, trying not to show the dread which swelled through his spirit.

Crawling over to him, Phineas implored, "Master, not to know is worse than all my imaginings. Do not spare me!"

Joseph looked into the eyes of his beloved friend, and studied the dear countenance which had always warmed him.

"God be with you, Phineas," he replied, "it is not happy news." Seeing that Phineas would bear no refusal, he sighed. "This is the interpretation: The three baskets

are three days. Within three days Pharaoh will lift up
your head...from off you. And will hang you upon a
tree."

Joseph's face was flushed, and tears spilled down his
cheeks. The baker, scarcely hearing him, at first chuck-
led.

But his master was not joking. As the reality of the
pronouncement flooded over him, he could not doubt,
as Tophet had. In his heart and spirit, which belonged to
Jehovah, he sensed that his kinsman spoke the truth.

"And the birds...Master. What are they doing?"

"Phineas," Joseph groaned. "You do not want to know."

"Speak, Master. Not to know is worse than all my
imaginings."

Phineas shivered under Joseph's scrutiny.

"Friend, you know the interpretation," the younger
surmised. "You know that in dreams, flesh and bread are
the same."

"Surely, Master, you cannot mean..."

Joseph said no more, longing to embrace him.

When he reached for him, however, Phineas drew
back.

"Touch me not, Master!" the baker cried. "For I am a
dead man! In three days shall the birds pick the skin from
off my bones!"

Joseph wept with him, and presently Phineas was
clutching at him, rocking to and fro. "It is so, is it not?
Tell me, so that I will think no worse!"

"It is so, Phineas," the Hebrew conceded. "In three
days...in three days..."

# 36

Upon the third day, Pharaoh Timaeus sat in his great chair, his elbows on his knees and his chin in his hands. Never had his counselors seen him so dejected, or so troubled.

Potiphera, who had been with him through the dreadful weeks since the revolution had begun, made helpless incantations to the gods for the health of the king and for the welfare of the nation. But by the sounds of the warfare in the streets, the Hyksos were gaining the upper hand.

It was Pharaoh's birthday and should have been a merry time in the mansion. But no one was celebrating. In fact, whenever any of the king's friends tried to do him a kindness, he scowled and sent them away.

The man who had replaced Tophet as the emperor's cupbearer kept a safe distance. Often he was called upon to fill the king's cup, for Pharaoh was drinking more than usual. But the new cupbearer had never pleased him.

"Draw the blinds!" the king shouted, sending the hapless fellow to the window. Doubtless Timaeus hoped to muffle the sounds of fighting and screaming in the boulevard. But the heavy draperies did not help, and the cupbearer met with further disapproval.

"Imbecile!" the king roared. "Potiphar," he called, using the priest's nickname, "where did you get this oaf?"

"He is one of your company, sir," the high priest reminded him. "He comes from the palace in Memphis."

Pharaoh did not like to be corrected, but Potiphera was his closest ally.

Softening, he looked through bleary eyes at the priest. "Who was that fellow who used to serve me here?" he wondered. "Fine fellow. Fine. Whatever became of him?"

Potiphera was concerned for the king's mind. Rising, he stepped behind his chair and began to massage the monarch's temples. As the emperor sank back, so that his head rested in his friend's hands, he drifted sleepily, wine and worry having taken too much toll.

"Do you not recall, My Lord?" the priest said. "He angered you, he and his chief baker."

Through a fog, the memory returned. And the king sighed, his vinegar breath filling the close space between himself and Potiphera.

"Potiphar..." he said affectionately, "I incarcerated the scoundrels, didn't I?"

"Indeed," the priest affirmed, sadly remembering his own harsh judgment against Joseph.

"Well, send for him," the king decided, his tongue heavy with drink. "I would have him serve me again."

"Then, it is fitting that we should have a feast, a birthday feast, after all!" the priest suggested, determined to cheer him.

"Very well," Timaeus nodded.

"And shall I call for the baker, too?" he hoped.

"Indeed, the baker, too." Pharaoh smiled. "Let the fool think he is being restored. And then," he said, carelessly flicking his hand as though to swat at a soulless fly, "when he is merry, behead him."

\* \* \*

Joseph stood mute in the corridor of the prison house, clutching at the ache in his chest.

Down the hall were the departing shadows of Pharaoh's guards, as they led away Tophet and Phineas.

"Remember the Lord," he had said, as Phineas was taken from him.

The butler, blithe of spirit, had gladly followed the men who came for him. But the baker, knowing they lied when they said he would be set free, had said nothing, only clinging to Joseph in terror.

Now Joseph was alone, abandoned as in the cistern, wondering how Jehovah could allow this, wondering why Phineas, kindest man in Egypt, must die.

Like a tourniquet, sorrow wrapped itself around Joseph's throat, and desperately he gasped for air. Turning, he headed for the black cell where he had spent so many hours in Phineas's presence, and once there, he threw himself upon the blanket pile where the baker had often sat.

Like a little child, he wrapped the blankets about him and tried not to cry.

But the tears would not be restrained. Weeping, he remembered all of his loved ones, and a pall of loneliness swept over him.

It was in this condition that Asenath found him hours later. Hours of seeking and asking after him.

She knew he would be mourning, for she knew the baker was his friend. And when she at last discovered him in the cell, she entered over the objections of the guards, over the objections of Joseph himself.

Sitting on the floor beside him, she drew near and cradled his head upon her breast.

This was yet another cave of Peniel. But this time, Asenath was Joseph's angel.

# PART V
# The Savior

# 37

Another full year of fighting had made the streets of On used to blood, as well as the streets of Memphis and every other Egyptian city. Peace was but a memory as victory favored first one side and then the other.

At last the stalwart Semites with their wild spirit won out over the weaker city-dwellers, and a Hyksos king took the throne.

The new Pharaoh, whose name was Salatis, had radical ideas and youthful vigor. Honoring the religion of the people, he allowed Potiphera to keep his position, but monotheism gained a foothold, and the simpler faith of the desert grew in popularity.

At his palace in Memphis, Salatis retained the best of his predecessor's servants and sent the rest away. Among those he kept for himself was Tophet, who served as his cupbearer in the stateroom of the empire's capital.

The politics of this new Pharaoh were far more liberal than those of the Theban Pharaohs. Although the conservatives had fought long and hard to retain the old ways, the people quickly came to love their new king, and by the time he was ready to celebrate his first anniversary upon the throne, the past had been forgotten.

So too had Joseph been forgotten. Tophet, in his restored position, had never seen the advantage of speaking to the old Pharaoh about the Hebrew. Though he now knew that Joseph was a prophet, and that he was gifted with unusual powers, Tophet thought it in his own best interest to let him stay where he was.

Under the new administration, there was even less reason for the cupbearer to consider the Hebrew who had served so well in Potiphera's house. Likely a Semite Pharaoh would have jumped at the chance to free him, and soon he would have been Tophet's superior again. In time, the butler conveniently forgot he had ever known such a fellow.

Pharaoh Salatis's first anniversary had just come and gone. Tophet's duties as chief cupbearer and butler in the Memphis palace were quite similar to those he had managed in On. For days he had borne a mountain of responsibility.

This morning his schedule was freer, and he was light-hearted as he headed for Pharaoh's chamber, ready to serve morning tea. Humming to himself as he passed down the hall, he considered his lot one of the happiest on earth and himself one of the most fortunate of men. No small salary was his as the king's attendant. A spacious apartment had been provided, and he always dressed in the finest of clothes. If a bit of conscience ever pricked him, he was able to suppress it; and he rarely thought on the sadder times he had seen.

As he rounded the corner of the hall nearest the king's chamber, he was not surprised to hear the sound of many voices arising from the room.

Tophet was used to finding counselors and servants in Pharaoh's bedroom. Salatis was not a shy fellow and often received visitors while still propped on his pillows. As his valets shaved and dressed him, he would discuss matters of state at hours when the heads of other nations would have preferred to sleep.

But the people gathered today in the chamber were unfamiliar to Tophet. Strange was their appearance— long-bearded fellows garbed in flowing gowns. Their garments were covered with occult symbols, and upon their wide belts were amulets of bone, hide, gold, and wood.

Though Tophet had never met these men, he recognized instantly that they must be the caste of magicians and seers who inhabited the capital's priestly monastery.

When he entered the room, they were consulting together, heads shaking, beards wagging. Tophet noted Pharaoh's frustrated expression as he listened to their reasonings.

As soon as Salatis addressed the butler, the crowd fell silent, studying him cautiously.

"It is all right, friends," Pharaoh said. "This is my cupbearer. Come, come, Tophet, do not be shy. Perhaps you can shed some light on this matter. Heaven knows you could do no worse than these 'wise men.' "

Surprised at the flattery, Tophet set down his tray and listened.

"I have had a dream," Salatis explained. "A troublesome one, indeed. And it seems no one in all this learned company has the interpretation." At this he leaned forward. "Tell me, Tophet, do you believe dreams have significance?"

The butler's mouth went dry. Uncomfortably he remembered his own dream and the marvelous interpretation which the imprisoned Hebrew had given.

"Sir . . . I do," he admitted.

"Very well!" Salatis enthused. Then gesturing dramatically to his embarrassed magi, he smirked, "So do they! But they stumble over the meaning of my vision. Help me, Tophet."

"Why, Your Majesty," the butler deferred, feigning humility, "who am I that I should overstep these powerful men? I surely am no seer."

At this Pharaoh began to laugh, hilariously holding his sides.

"That is very good, Tophet," he said, slapping the butler on the back. "This occasion can use some humor. No, no, dear Tophet, I was hoping that perhaps since you once dwelt in the house of the high priest, you might have heard of some seer, some wise man who has been overlooked."

Blushing, Tophet cleared his throat, feeling suddenly foolish.

For the first time in months, Joseph haunted him as surely as though he hovered in a corner of the room. Guilt speared the butler's heart, and with a shudder he tried to blunt it.

"Well, Your Highness," he stuttered, "I shall give it some thought. Indeed, I shall."

Then, bowing, he proceeded to pour the tea, wishing Salatis would not eye him with such curiosity.

When at last the conversation recommenced in the room, and when Pharaoh's attention was diverted, Tophet's trembling eased and his heart slowed a bit.

Still, Joseph's face haunted him, and he recalled his pleas to remember him when he gained his liberty.

In keeping with Tophet's nature, however, he would consider his own interests above all others'. At first, as he did so, it seemed risky to mention the Hebrew. But the more he thought, the more he realized that if he could be responsible for bringing an answer to Pharaoh's riddle, he might be advanced as never before.

The wheels in Tophet's mind turned quickly. He would tell this king he had once worked with the lad in Potiphera's house, and that Joseph had been thrown into prison even though he had a reputation as a seer.

But, no. What if the king sent for Joseph, and Joseph, in turn, mentioned Tophet's imprisonment?

The butler nervously handed the master his tea, grateful that the king was preoccupied so that he did not study Tophet's tense face too closely.

It seemed if he spoke of Joseph at all, he must speak of his own time in jail. But if he did, the king would surely doubt his character altogether, strip him of his rank, and send him away.

Back and forth he debated the matter until it struck

him that there might be a safe way to tell the truth, a way which could actually be advantageous to him.

"Sir," he said softly, "it occurs to me that I may be able to help."

"Yes?" the king said, almost having forgotten Tophet's presence.

"In doing so, I must confess my own offenses. For it involves a sorry time in my life."

Not a little surprised, the emperor and his companions were intrigued.

"You know that your predecessor was a ruthless and unjust ruler," Tophet began, as though contrasting the old administration with the new.

What could the new king do, but agree? When he nodded, Tophet went on.

"Pharaoh was furious with his servants, and he put me in confinement in the house of the captain of the bodyguard, both me and the chief baker. We both had dreams on the same night, and we were troubled by them."

"Go on," Salatis encouraged him.

"Now a Hebrew youth was with us there, a servant of the captain of the bodyguard, and we related our dreams to him, and he interpreted them for us."

Allowing suspense to build, Tophet paused.

"Amazingly, it came about that just as he interpreted for us, so it happened. Pharaoh restored me to my office, but the baker he hanged."

With this, he rolled his eyes and gripped his neck as with a noose, adding drama to the fine tale.

Momentarily the room was abuzz again, as the magi wondered over the mysterious soothsayer.

Salatis stroked his beard and looked quietly at Tophet. Pleased with the story, he announced, "If my cupbearer was an enemy to Timaeus, then he is an honest man. And if this prisoner of whom he speaks is a Hebrew, he must be a true prophet. Send for him that we may all be satisfied."

# 38

Slick as a Nile breeze, the wheels of a flashing carriage sped to the Memphis acropolis.

From between the parted curtains a beaming face peered, the face of the long-imprisoned Joseph.

For two years his greatest freedom had been his daily trek from the fortress apartment provided by Potiphera to the jailhouse in the prison of On. Though he had been "keeper of the prison," he had still been a ward of the state, a criminal.

Today he was on his way to Pharaoh's palace, the only mansion in Egypt greater than Potiphera's. And today he would be welcomed into the stateroom of the new Semite king.

Something told him this was the Lord's day, which he had awaited since his dreadful casting off. This was the day when the prophecies of his youth would begin to be fulfilled.

He was thirty years old and as handsome as a desert prince—for so he was, a prince of the line of Abraham. Perhaps, even this he could shortly reveal, the pride of his heritage and the faith of his fathers.

He could still smell Asenath's sweet perfume as she had hovered over him this morning, eagerly offering her assistance as he prepared to leave.

Personally bringing word of Pharaoh's summons, she had also arrived at his apartment bearing a stack of garments, fine linen embellished with finer accessories.

With her were her maids, carrying trays of male toiletries: a razor, comb, mirror, cologne, and soap.

Laughing and giggling, the women had handed him tunics and cloaks and had made him come out to them in outfit after outfit.

"There," Asenath had at last announced, "the striped one suits you best."

He had not told her he knew it would. He had not revealed that he had once worn a coat of many colors, simpler but more stunning than this.

Ahead, against capitol hill, the palace of the king loomed.

"A dream . . ." Joseph thought. "The king has had a dream, and he calls for me."

When Pharaoh's messengers had arrived in On, seeking Joseph, they had not mentioned Tophet. But Joseph knew there could be no other explanation for the summons. A smirk worked at Joseph's lips as he thought about the selfish butler. It must be that Tophet now served under the new administration, and that he had good personal reason to suddenly remember the Hebrew.

As the chariot dashed through the mammoth gate of the palace compound, Joseph took a deep breath. He could suddenly feel the past slipping from him, sluffed like a worn-out garment.

A bright future beckoned, and he would receive it with eager hands.

\* \* \*

The spacious halls of Pharaoh Salatis's castle echoed about Joseph as he followed the messengers toward the king's stateroom. He had always thought the house of On must be the most magnificent on earth. But nothing could rival the majesty of this place.

Once they had passed the tight security stations which introduced the first lobbies, they entered the inner sanctums, where spilling fountains and exotic birds greeted guests, where gorgeous women lounged in garden bowers, and where music drifted on warm currents from corners and alcoves.

Rich tapestries caressed the walls and thick carpets the floors. Mirrors reflected the reality that he was indeed here, that although he was an interpreter of dreams, this was no dream.

Over and over he breathed a prayer, the same one he had repeated since leaving On. It was a prayer for wisdom and insight, a prayer that Jehovah would facilitate his calling and help him to perceive the meaning of Pharaoh's troubling vision.

Confidence in God had carried him from the dungeon, across the miles to Memphis, and through the awesome corridors of this place. Now he stood before the stateroom door. Clenching his fists, he imagined that he clung to Jehovah's unfailing hand.

It was a tall, thin man with bead-like eyes who opened the portal, greeting Joseph with a diverted gaze. Blood rushed to the visitor's face as he recognized the butler.

He knew not whether to embrace Tophet or shun him.

"Enter, Master," the man greeted, unable to face the one he should have freed from prison months before.

"It has been a long time, Tophet," Joseph returned.

Saying nothing more, he entered, walking tall and silent into the stateroom.

Ahead, upon a vast marble platform, sat the king. As Joseph was announced to him, he was not surprised to find that the new Pharaoh was a young man, younger even than himself. He had expected such a revolutionary hero to be full of youthful zeal. Nor was Joseph surprised to see that he was dark and ruddy, like the desert race from which he was descended.

In fact, the new Pharaoh could have passed for a nomad prince, which likely he was before taking the mightiest throne on earth.

Tall and dashing, he appeared bred on mountain air and stream water, and when the son of Jacob stood before him, the two men instantly recognized one another.

It was not a recognition borne of knowledge, but of spirit. They were of the same stock—Semites, Hebrews, people of the earth. And they must have cut their teeth on the same stones.

"Joseph," Salatis called out, "that is an Aramaean name, is it not?"

"Yes, Your Majesty," the Hebrew replied. "I was born in Padan-Aram."

In that instant he revealed more about his heritage than he had told anyone since setting foot in Egypt. And over the next moments he found himself revealing more.

"My people hark back to Mesopotamia," Pharaoh said.

"Mine, as well," Joseph answered. "My great-grand-father was a prince of Ur."

Stunned, the king leaned forward, studying his handsome visitor in amazement.

"I almost believe you," he marveled. "You look the part."

Joseph would have been flattered, but knew the truth of the statement and sensed Pharaoh's sincerity.

"Tell me of your tribe and your god," the king inquired.

With this, Joseph recounted his story, his lineage, and how he had come to be first a slave and then a steward in Potiphera's house. Before he knew it, he had related the encounter with Natira. All of this Salatis accepted without question.

"My God is the God of my fathers: Abraham, Isaac, and Jacob," he reverently concluded. "It is my God who has kept me all these years, and who will answer for me this day."

The king sighed, a smile lighting his face. "I have heard this kind of talk before, among the desert people. It gives me peace to hear it again."

Joseph thrilled to this confession. Suddenly he felt an even deeper bond with this man, and a desire to serve him the best he could.

"Now as to the reason I have called for you, Joseph," Salatis began, "I have had a dream, and I know it to be the kind of dream which means to tell me something. I cannot put it from mind, but no one can interpret it. I have heard it said that when *you* hear a dream you can interpret it."

Joseph bowed, feeling Tophet's eyes against his back.

"It is not in me to be so wise," he admitted. "It is God who gives me the understanding. And God will give Pharaoh a favorable answer this day."

This pleased the king greatly, relieving him of a heavy burden.

"Very well," he said. Then closing his eyes, he recounted the vision:

"In my dream, I was standing on the bank of the Nile. Suddenly seven cows, fat and sleek, came up out of the river. They grazed in the marsh grass which grew there. Then, seven other cows came up after them, poor and very ugly and gaunt, uglier than any I had ever seen in all the land of Egypt."

He shivered a little, as though the dream still terrified him.

"Then the lean, ugly cows ate up the first seven fat ones. Oh, it was horrible, Joseph! Yet when they had devoured them, it didn't look as though they had, for they were just as ugly and skinny as before."

At this, he opened his eyes and shook himself.

Joseph wondered if this were all, and began to consider an answer, but the king was not finished.

"I awoke for a space, but then fell asleep again," he went on. "And the dream continued. This time seven ears of grain, plump and good, came up on a single stalk. And then, seven more, withered, thin, and scorched by the east wind, sprouted up after them. The thin ears swallowed the seven good ears."

Pharaoh's voice trailed off, and his hands shook. Rubbing them together as though they were cold, he held them forth, desperate.

"Joseph, I told my dream to the magi, but no one could explain it to me. If you can help, I shall reward you beyond your wildest imaginings!"

Joseph understood that Salatis felt the dream portentous of the future, and that as ruler of Egypt he feared for his country.

But though the vision was deep and obscure, the meaning came to the Hebrew like a quick wind off the hills of Lebanon.

"The two parts of the dream have the same meaning," he began. "God is telling you what he is about to do."

"Truly?" the king marveled. "I have known this. Yes, yes!"

"The seven good cows are seven years," the interpreter explained. "Likewise the seven healthy ears of grain. Do you see?"

"I see, I see! Go on."

"The seven thin cows and the seven thin ears scorched by the east wind are also seven years . . . of famine."

The king lurched forward. "This is not good," he observed. "There will be famine in Egypt?"

"It is as I have spoken," Joseph insisted. "God has shown you what he is about to do. Now, understand. Seven years of great abundance are coming, but they shall be followed by seven more years of famine, and all of the abundance will be forgotten, for the famine will ravage the land. In fact the wealth of the first seven shall be devoured by the last."

The Hebrew let the message sink into his hearer's ears. And when he saw that Salatis resisted, he said, "You had the dream twice because God is trying to warn you. He shall bring all this to happen very soon!"

The king shook his head. "But, Joseph, you said at the beginning that God would give me a favorable interpretation. This is not favorable. It is very foreboding."

"Don't you see?" Joseph went on. "It would be unfavorable if you received no warning. This way you will have time to prepare. If I were you, O Great King, I would seek a wise and discerning man to set in charge of these matters. Put overseers in charge of the land, and let them exact a fifth of the produce of all the farmland during the seven bounteous years. Let them gather that portion into the silos of every city, under the authority of the crown. Be sure to set guards over these reserves, and let no one partake of the supply during the seven healthy years, so that when the famine comes, there will be plenty."

As the king listened to the proposal, he was dumbfounded. Studying his visitor, he motioned to his counselors, who had stood quietly by throughout the discussion.

For a few moments they consulted together, looking over their shoulders now and then and eyeing Joseph in wonder. At last Salatis stood up.

"Can we ever find such a fellow again?" he asked, gesturing to the Hebrew. "This Joseph, son of Jacob, has a divine spirit!"

Then calling Joseph forward, he proclaimed, "Since God has informed you of all this, there is no one so discerning or wise as you! I summoned you for an interpretation, and you not only gave me that, but you gave me wise counsel as well! As of this day, I put you in charge of my entire palace and all that concerns me. At your command, all my people shall do homage. Only I, in all of Egypt, shall be greater than you!"

As Joseph stood spellbound before him, the king stepped down from his platform, removed his signet ring, and put it on Joseph's hand. Then, sending for a linen cloak, he wrapped it about Joseph's shoulders and put a golden necklace about his neck.

"Zaphenath-paneah," Salatis proclaimed, kissing him on both cheeks. "So shall your name be from this day. For through you does God speak and through you he shows that he lives."

# 39

Joseph, prime minister of Egypt, stood in the spur of his chariot, a stinging whip flashing in his hand. Four elegant stallions, white as Hebron snow, pulled to the chase of his command.

Behind him, within the chariot, stood two princely young boys, one six years old, and one five.

Manasseh, he had named the first; and Ephraim, the youngest; for the first had helped him to forget the past and the second was proof of his fruitfulness in the land of his affliction.

Both were blessed with Joseph's ruddy good looks, but lavender glinted in their eyes, and their mother's smooth Egyptian features gave them refined dignity even at this early age.

They were the offspring of Asenath and Joseph, born in due time after Pharaoh had given her in marriage to the Hebrew.

While the union required that Asenath give up her position as priestess of Nath, Potiphera could not deny his blessing on the couple. Loving Joseph like a son and still feeling the guilt of his past treatment of him, he provided a grand wedding, one of the most elaborate ever staged in Egypt.

And as Asenath grew in her devotion to the God of Israel, Joseph knew bliss more profound than anything he dreamed could be his.

The first year of famine was upon the land, coming just

as the Hebrew had predicted after seven full years of plenty.

During the times of abundance, Joseph had traveled back and forth throughout Egypt, overseeing the fulfillment of his plan, the ingathering of a fifth of all agricultural products and the storing up of grain and dried foods in every city silo.

Because the new emperor was so popular, Joseph's edict was followed from the beginning with little resistance. And as time proved, he was indeed a prophet, for the seven fruitful years were in themselves miraculously abundant.

Today as he entered the border town of Succoth, on the east side of Egypt, he was greeted by cheers; and as he passed down the avenue, his attendants, riding on before, called out, *"Abreck! Abreck!* Attention! Attention! All bow!"

Anticipating the prime minister's arrival, the people complied, eagerly gathering along the street and in the marketplace.

All nations were represented among them, for the famine had spread throughout the known world, touching the edge of western Africa and the borders of India, the realms of southern Europe and the desert of Mesopotamia.

In all the earth, no land had food except Egypt. And Pharaoh himself would have been starving, had the wise Hebrew and his God-given prophecy not been heeded.

In every city of the land, the scene was similar when Joseph arrived. Wealthy and poor alike waited to buy food from the storehouses.

Those who had everything money could offer, except nourishment, mingled with people who had spent their last reserves just to make the journey to Egypt.

Strange dialects mixed, as well as strange clothing, the sarongs of west Africans contrasting with the streamlined robes of the Europeans and the turbans of the desert people. Black, white, and brown faces stared up at Joseph as he took his seat beneath an awning on an elevated platform and prepared to open the market.

Much of the food had set prices, but there were those people who wished to buy in such quantity that great lots of the products would be auctioned.

More than once had Joseph considered the irony of his situation: that he, once a piece of merchandise upon a slave block, should now be master of life and death in the greatest bazaar of all time.

But he took no joy in the neediness of those who came before him. Joseph knew what it was to suffer, to be poor and powerless, at the mercy of others. Day after day his heart was broken by the poverty and helplessness of the thousands who came in waves, bowing and seeking salvation.

Today, as his young sons stood by watching his attendants take silver, gold, precious stones, and personal treasures in exchange for grain and dried foods, Joseph recalled the times he had wished he might have something to offer in exchange for his freedom. As the clerks in the accounting booths kept scrupulous record of every transaction, committing it to clay tablet and parchment, he remembered the heartless men who had looked upon him as in item of barter and profit.

But most often these days, he thought of his brothers, and he wondered how they fared in the land of Canaan, so hard hit by famine.

One of Joseph's accountants had just handed him a figure-laden tablet, and after he approved it, he reached for another.

Just as he did, a certain company within the great throng caught Joseph's attention.

At first he thought his eyes deceived him, that it was only in the context of his thoughts that he would imagine such a thing. But the more he studied them, the more his heart raced.

Calling his sons to his side, he wrapped an arm around each one and, trembling, held them close. The lads, not knowing what possessed their father, surveyed the crowd but did not see what he saw.

"Papa?" Manasseh began to question him.

Joseph held a finger to his lips. "Tell me, son," he whispered, "do I look Egyptian today?"

The two boys giggled. "You will do," Manasseh teased.

"Quickly," the Hebrew told him, "go fetch my head-dress."

"But, Papa," Manasseh objected, "it is too hot to wear that today."

"Quickly," Joseph spurred him.

When the boy returned with the broad, striped head-piece, Joseph donned it. "Do I look Egyptian?" he asked again.

"Yes, Papa," Ephraim assured him. "But why..."

"Run along now, sons," Joseph commanded. "Your mother should be arriving soon."

Asenath was due to join him, as she often did when he was away. But he did not want his wife and children to see him just now.

As the boys departed, their faces quizzical, Joseph turned again to his work, hoping that the men who now approached the platform would not recognize him.

There were exactly ten of them, and in the 20 years which had passed since last he saw them, they had changed little.

The leader was only more mature, his distinguished beard laced with silver. Joseph knew on the instant that he was Reuben.

Behind him came Judah, his intelligent face a little mellower with age. Then there were the two "lions," Simeon and Levi, although Joseph was surprised to find them not much taller than himself.

Benjamin, Joseph's eleventh and only full brother, was nowhere among them.

As they came forward, giving homage, tears rose in the Hebrew's eyes. The visions of the bowing sheaves and obeisant stars sprang to mind as though he had witnessed them just yesterday, and not when he was a boy.

Gripping the arms of his chair, he controlled himself, determined not to reveal his feelings.

Calling for a clean ledger, he pretended to take notes.

"Where do you come from?" he asked with the rough air of command.

Though the children of Israel knew the Egyptian tongue he spoke, it was polite to let his interpreter translate. When the question had been recast in Hebrew, it was Reuben who answered, keeping his face to the ground.

"From the land of Canaan, sir. To buy food."

"Is the famine so severe in that lush land?" Joseph tested him. Having contrived a plot to detain them, he suddenly sneered, "I suspect you are all heads of nomad tribes, here to spy out the borders of our country!"

Reuben looked up in amazement and confusion, and turning to Judah, shrugged his shoulders.

"Good sir," he said, bowing again, "permit your servant to disagree. Surely there have been many from Canaan seeking your help. The famine is very harsh in our country. We are not spies. No, my lord, but to buy food are your servants come."

"Yes, sir," Judah added, rising up and pleading, "we are all the sons of one man. We are honest men, not spies."

Joseph pretended skepticism, unwilling to expose himself, yet gleaning what information he could regarding the family.

"The sons of one man?" he laughed. "How likely is that? Look around you. Do you see so many men traveling in company? All well dressed, all strong and young? No, no. You are spies!"

At this Simeon came forth, ready to fight, his face as red as his beard.

"Sir," he argued, stupidly adding more detail, "not only are your servants ten brothers, but all together there are twelve of us, the sons of one man in Canaan!"

When the other brothers nudged him to keep quiet, Simeon only made matters worse. "The youngest is at home with our father," he stammered, "and the other . . . is not."

The last observation stuck in Simeon's throat, and Joseph noted how the ten men appeared uneasy with it.

Again, emotion welled within the inquisitor, but he feigned indifference.

"So, indeed, you have a father? And another brother?"

Judah, who studied the governor quizzically, sighed. "Yes, sir. It is as we have said. We have a father, an old man, and a child of his old age, a little one. And the child's brother is dead, and . . . his father loves him."

"Little One . . ." the words pricked Joseph's heart, for so had he been called by that name during all his years at home. But steeling himself against sentiment, he snorted, "Ha! A likely story! You strain my patience! It is as I suspected. You are all spies!"

At this he stood up and began to pace his platform. His attendants nervously called the guards, and the huge market crowd gasped in astonishment.

As weapon-bearing strong men surrounded the small company, fear clouded the ten faces.

"To show that I am a just man," Joseph condescended, "I shall give you a chance to prove yourselves."

Reuben gripped the edge of the platform. "Anything, sir, for we are honest men."

"Very well," Joseph continued, pacing to and fro. "This shall be your proof: By the life of Pharaoh, you shall not leave this place unless your youngest brother comes to Egypt."

The ten Israelites murmured together, shaking their heads and insisting that this was impossible, that their old father would surely die if the lad were to leave him.

But Joseph insisted. "Send one of you to fetch your brother. The rest shall be kept in confinement until I see if you are telling the truth! Otherwise, by the life of Pharaoh, you are surely spies!"

Quaking and trembling, the ten cried out as the guards bound them and hauled them away.

And Joseph left the platform, tears brimming in his eyes.

# 40

Asenath peeked through the flap of her husband's striped tent. Despite the searing daylight outside, the heavy shelter was dark inside, and she called softly, wondering where he was.

When he did not answer, she crept through the door and tiptoed to his couch.

The crowd of hungry marketers waited beside the platform for the prime minister to return, but Joseph had not come out of his traveling tent since committing the Israelites to prison.

A full hour had passed while heat and hunger made the people restless, and a threatening chant rose from the street.

"Husband," Asenath whispered, finding him sprawled face down upon his bed. "What are you doing here? Manasseh and Ephraim are worried. The people..."

Joseph reached for her through the dark and pulled her to him.

Still he said nothing, but when she stroked his face, she found his cheeks wet with tears.

"My lord, what has happened?" she cried. "Is there no more food? Shall the people starve?"

"No, no," he soothed her. "I am coming. Tell them I am coming."

Asenath rose to do as he asked, but he pulled her to him again.

"My heart breaks, Asenath. I have seen my brothers,

the ten who left me for dead!"

"Here? In Succoth?" she marveled.

"All the way from Cannan."

"But how can you be sure? It is so many years."

"I knew them all," he insisted. "They are so unchanged!"

Asenath sat quiet beside him a long moment, stroking his forehead and feeling what he felt.

Knowing Joseph as she did, she knew compassion would overrule vengeance. For this man, she had recanted her previous faith, giving up her devotion to the gods of Egypt and embracing the faith of Israel. Never had she regretted her choice, and never had she doubted her husband's wisdom.

"Well," she sighed, "you have power now, husband. Their lives are in your hands."

"Yes," he muttered. "Just as they should be!"

"Just as they should be," she repeated, a smile tugging at her mouth. "So what do you mean to do?"

"I have had them hauled away to prison!" he asserted, a little too strongly.

"I see," she said. "And shall they rot there forever?"

Silence, like smoke, hung between them.

"What would *you* do?" he challenged. "Surely you would do no less!"

"I would do exactly what you would do," she replied.

Joseph hated the lilt in her voice, the teasing twinkle in her eye that reached through the dark into his heart.

He hated Asenath and loved her, both at once.

* * *

This was the second night that Joseph could not sleep.

Two days had passed since he had encountered his brothers, days of doling out food to strangers, of seeing fear and starvation exchanged for gratitude and hope.

But his conscience tormented him.

A luscious yellow moon hovered over the border town and some desert wolf serenaded it. Asenath breathed softly beside her husband, confident that he would make the right decision. He should have been at peace, but he was not.

Somewhere across town, in a primitive hold, his ten brothers were probably also awake, fearing for their lives and wondering if they would ever see Canaan or Jacob again.

Conflicting emotions—joy at seeing them, unresolved anger at their abuses—contended for Joseph's heart.

Several times since the Israelites had appeared he had thought to pray. But each time he had rebelled, preferring to nurse his dark memories.

As dawn approached, he knew he could not spend another day in indecision. He also knew what his move must be, for the sake of his own soul.

Before the sun had cracked the sky, Joseph was on his feet, creeping out of the tent and leaving the slumbering Asenath without a word.

Rousing his interpreter, he led him to the prison-house, which was no more than a stockade of stakes and armed guards. Shivering with desert cold, he stood outside while the bewildered spokesman called the brothers to the door.

The Israelites came forward in a huddle, rubbing their eyes and muttering together.

"Tell them I fear the same God they fear," Joseph began, nudging the servant. "Tell them that if they wish to live and if they are honest men, they must leave one of their brothers behind. The rest may carry food to their families. But they must all return as quickly as possible with their youngest brother. If they do this, they shall live."

As the men absorbed the message, Joseph watched their faces. Relief was there, but fear as well.

"We must leave one of us here?" he heard them ask. "And we must return again to Egypt?"

The interpreter nodded, and Joseph knew their quandary.

How could they single out one brother to remain? And how could they expect Jacob to release Benjamin to an unknown fate?

What, they wondered among themselves, could this Zaphenath-paneah want with the lad? And how could Jacob, aged and frail, survive such separation?

All this they discussed among themselves, not realizing that Joseph perfectly understood their tongue.

They could not seem to reach a consensus before they began to cast about for some rhyme or reason for their predicament.

Doubtless they had gone over and over it before, the peculiar treatment they were receiving, and why this strange Egyptian should suspect them as he did.

No satisfactory answer had come after two days and nights of deliberation, and now they were left with nothing but the sense that they were being divinely punished.

"Oh," Levi wailed, "it is as I have always feared. We are being repaid for our sin against Joseph!"

"You see that now?" Judah snarled. "I knew from the beginning that we should have been kinder to the lad."

"Ha!" Gad barked. "You were ready to sell him! What could be more cruel?"

"So? What about *you*?" Judah defended. "You were ready to *kill* him!"

At this Gad started, and pointing at Asher recalled how he had committed Joseph to the pit.

But Asher turned on them all. "We saw Joseph's agony when he pleaded with us, yet none of us would listen! I am no more to blame than you all!"

On and on the argument went, until Reuben spoke up. "I agree that it is because of this great sin that this evil has come upon us! Did I not warn you, 'Do not sin against the boy'? Yet you would not take heed. Now comes the reckoning for his blood!"

Joseph's chest tightened, and he grew short of breath. Turning aside, he left the compound and stood in the moonlit shadows.

Years of repressed sorrow welled from within, and like a young child, he wept until his confounded interpreter came seeking him.

"Master!" he exclaimed. "What is it?"

Shoving the man away, Joseph got control of himself and returned to the stockade, commanding the guards to let him in.

To the amazement of all, he began to bark orders.

"Since you cannot seem to choose, *I* shall do so!" he cried.

Grasping Simeon by the arms, he took a silken rope from off his own waist and proceeded to bind the big fellow's hands behind his back.

With this gesture, something close to a sense of vengeance swept over Joseph. As he recalled Simeon's sins at Shechem, his cruel and prideful destruction of the town of Shalem and his humiliation of their sister, Dinah, he bound him rudely.

"This one shall stay," he decided, "and the rest of you shall go! Bring your youngest brother with all speed, or surely you shall not live long!"

Then, storming out, he commanded the guards to free the nine, and he turned for his tent.

When he was half-way home, his interpreter racing to keep pace, Joseph suddenly felt an ache in his chest. Stopping, he braced himself against a lamppost and closed his eyes.

The anguish of conflict consumed him. Running a hand over his brow, he sighed deeply.

Overhead the moon watched as Joseph swung between hate and love.

"See to it that they are well supplied with grain," he instructed the interpreter. "And while you are at it, restore all the money that they pay. Hide it in their bags. And send them away."

# 41

The inn at Beer-Sheba was a desolate place. Dry breezes withered what little vegetation the desert produced, creating huge tumbleweeds that could threaten the sturdiest horse or camel.

But this was the southernmost outpost of the land of Canaan, the first true resting place for travelers crossing the Wilderness of Shur or the Wilderness of Zin from Egypt and points south.

Hundreds of people were lodged here this evening, all on their way to or from the land of Pharaoh, all going after food or bringing food back with them.

Judah pushed against a blast of desert sand on his way from the inn to the stable. He had fed his donkey the last of a bag of meal just before bedtime, but the poor beast was still hungry and he could hear it braying in the moonlit yard.

Reaching the stable, he rubbed the donkey between the ears, and chastised him gently. "Petri, your stomach is bottomless!" he complained. "I didn't want to open a new bag until morning. Shall you eat up our supplies before we reach home?"

The stubborn creature brayed again as Judah loosened the drawstring on a sack of oats and dipped his hand inside.

When the Israelite stubbed his fingers on something hard, he foraged in the bag, his brow crinkled.

"What's this?" he asked, pulling out a leather pouch.

The donkey studied it blankly as Judah shook it, listening to the jangling contents.

"My purse!" he exclaimed. "See here, Petri, it is my purse!"

Nervously, Judah opened the bag and, turning it over, found that his money was all there, the money he had paid for his supplies.

At first the realization made him giddy as he marveled at his good fortune. It seemed some oversight on the part of the stockkeepers in Succoth had fallen to his benefit.

As he considered further, however, rubbing the coins in his hands, fear seized him. Replacing the money in the pouch, he dropped it into the sack and hastily covered it over.

Like a criminal, he fled back to the inn and roused his sleeping brothers.

"My money has been returned!" he told them, his voice as low as possible. "It is in my meal bag! When the prime minister learns that the payment is missing, he will be convinced that we are thieves!"

"And spies!" Asher cried, sitting up on his pallet.

Reuben listened mutely to his brothers' reasoning, as one by one they turned to him for guidance.

"Simeon is as good as dead!" Levi moaned. "Oh, Reuben, what is this that God has done to us?"

But Reuben had no answer, sensing that the Lord's justice was on an irreversible course.

* * *

A hot night wind parched the Hebron hills and scoured the settlement at Mamre.

Jacob paced the floor of the tribal council chamber, shaking his head in outrage.

"You did *what*?" he shouted. "You left Simeon in Succoth?"

"The governor of Egypt was against us," Reuben defended. So many times had he rehearsed the story to his father that his nerves were ready to shatter.

The nine brothers, who sat in a circle on the floor, wrung their hands in frustration.

"Yes, Father," Judah interceded, "listen to Reuben. We had no choice. This strange Egyptian took a disliking to us from the outset. We have gone over and over the possible reasons but have no answer. He simply decided from the moment he saw us that we were untrustworthy."

"Spies?" Jacob cried. "How could he think you spies?"

Again, the matter had been tossed about so many times that the men tired of it. But, revering Jacob, they went over it once more.

Back and forth the elder paced, listening, dissatisfied, angry.

"Well, the man is insane!" he declared. "You are all insane if you think I shall release Benjamin to you."

Stumbling across the room, he reached for the young man, the only remaining son of Rachel, who absorbed all of this in bewildered silence. Benjamin received his father's embrace without a word, ready to offer himself for the journey, but fearful lest he break the old man's heart.

"You have bereaved me of two sons already!" Jacob cried, turning on the others. "I left Joseph to your care and he is no more. Now Simeon is gone, and you would take Benjamin? You must think me a fool!"

"Papa, Papa..." Benjamin stammered. "Perhaps it is necessary..."

But before he could complete the thought, Jacob was raving again. Staggering to a corner of the chamber, the elder reached into a cedar chest and brought out the striped coat which had once been Joseph's.

Scattered upon it were deep crimson stains, the blood of a slain beast into which the brothers had dipped the garment years before, "proof" that the vanished Joseph had met with a violent and mysterious death in the wilderness.

Clutching the coat to his breast, Jacob began to weep.

"Father," Reuben pleaded, placing an arm about the old man's shoulders, "if we do not comply, the Egyptian will surely send troops after our entire tribe! Do not worry over Benjamin. I swear, you may put my own two sons to death if I do not bring him back safely. Put him in my care, and I *will* return him to you!"

Wrenching free, Jacob stared wildly into Reuben's compassionate face.

"My son shall not go down with you!" he growled. "Joseph, his only brother, is dead, and he alone is left. If harm should befall him on the journey, you will bring my gray hair down to the grave in sorrow!"

# 42

It was not his sons' persuasiveness that finally convinced Jacob to release Benjamin.

It was hunger—and it was fear.

As the food supply again dwindled, someone must return to the land of Pharaoh.

The predicament was compounded by the fact that, when the food sacks which they had brought with them from Egypt had been opened, each brother discovered that, like Judah, one of his bags contained his money. To return now, appearing as a batch of thieves, would surely put their lives in peril. But to delay could bring starvation, or the army of Pharaoh against Israel.

As Jacob saw that he had no choice but to comply with the prime ministers's orders, he finally permitted Benjamin to go.

"If it must be so," he decided, "then do this: Take some of the best products of our land in your bags, and carry them down to the governor as a gift. Take a little balm and a little honey, aromatic gum and myrrh, pistachio nuts and almonds. And take double the money in your hand which was found in your sacks. Perhaps...we will hope that perhaps it was an oversight."

Then, clasping Benjamin to himself, he handed him over to the care of Reuben and Judah.

"May God Almighty grant you compassion in the sight of the prime minster," he prayed. "As for me, if I am bereaved of my children...I am bereaved."

Therefore it was with much trepidation that the sons of Israel saw the walls of Succoth on the horizon, the dread place of their imprisonment and the town where the prime minster was still headquartered.

Was Simeon still alive, confined in the stockade?

Cautiously they made their way through the town gate, the most easterly portal of Egypt.

It was early morning when they arrived. The governor was just finishing breakfast on the porch of his great tent, his wife and sons lounging beside him.

Like a spear, it went through Joseph, the sight of his returning brothers. Lurching upright on his couch, he felt his face blanch, and without explanation he sent his little family away.

"Take your maidservants and our sons, and leave the house!" he commanded Asenath. "Do not return until evening."

Wounded by his sharp command, the woman was incredulous. But when she followed his gaze down the street, she saw for the first time the faces of his notorious persecutors, and understanding his desire to be alone, she hastened to obey.

Eagerly Joseph scanned the group which approached. Yes, there he was! Benjamin! He would know him anywhere!

Ecstasy and yearning gripped him. Benjamin was handsome as a mountain cedar—his beard and hair black as bark, his skin the same golden ivory and his eyes the same lavender as Rachel's. Suddenly Joseph was 17 again, and he rode through Hebron's heathered hills beside his little brother, laughing and free.

Somehow he managed to keep back the tears. Calling to his interpreter, he commanded, "Bring the men into the house, and slay a choice fatling. Make ready, for the men are to dine with me at noon!"

Remembering his master's previous suspicions of these very characters, the servant could barely refrain from questioning the order. But with a hesitant bow, he hurried down the street.

"You are to come with me," he announced, taking Reuben by the arm. "My lord would have you dine with him."

Of course, the Israelites recognized him as the governor's aide, and they imagined the hand of doom upon their shoulders.

Quaking, Levi dared to voice their fear.

"It is because of the money that we are being brought in," he muttered. "He will fall upon us and take us for slaves!"

"Hush!" Judah snarled. And those nearest Levi elbowed him to keep silent.

Rigidly they followed the servant to the edge of the porch. Taking a deep breath, Reuben drew close behind him.

"Oh, my lord," he offered, avoiding his gaze, "we did truly come here the first time to buy food. We had no other motive. But it so happened..." Fumbling, he explained that they had found the money in their bags and quickly related that they had brought more than enough in repayment.

"We do not know who put the money in our sacks," he added sincerely.

When the man reached out to touch him on the sleeve, Reuben froze, envisioning the end.

But the interpreter only smiled.

"Peace to you," he said. "Do not be afraid. Your God and the God of your father has given you treasure in your sacks."

Then, turning for the door, he called over his shoulder, "I had your money. Relax and enjoy, for the governor...heaven knows why...has taken favor on you."

# 43

For the Israelites, the next few hours were like a dream.

When the ten brothers were ushered into the small enclosure which served as Joseph's traveling courtyard, they were greeted by the aromas of a succulent meal. Arrayed beneath an awning were several long tables, all laden with trays of fine food and goblets of wine.

The interpreter, who also served as Joseph's steward, went on ahead of the men, disappearing for a few moments behind a tall screen. When he returned, he led a handsome, red-bearded giant, dressed in the finest clean linen.

"Simeon!" Levi cried. Rushing to him, he embraced him fervently.

"He has been released," the steward explained, seeing their astonishment. "Do not ask me why, for I do not know."

Then, shrugging his shoulders, he led the company toward the dining area.

The prime minister, they were told, had left the house on business and would be arriving at noon. Meanwhile, they were presented with fresh water and towels with which to wash their feet, faces, and hands. They were given clean tunics to wear and were entertained with music while their cups were filled over and over with spiced tea.

When at last the governor's arrival was announced, a small trumpet blaring in the court, the Israelites rose from their couches and prostrated themselves upon the floor.

Not one dared to look up, fearing the face of the peculiar Egyptian and fearing whatever he intended for them.

As Joseph stood upon his porch, surveying the obeisant brothers, he again remembered his visions and tried valiantly to suppress his welling emotions.

"Rise," he simply said. "Take your seats."

At this, the Israelites returned to their couches, all but Reuben, who rose only to his knees.

"Your Highness," he humbly replied, "if you will be patient with your servant, we have a gift from our homeland, prepared in your honor."

Joseph easily read the tension in his brother's voice, a fear equal to his own conflict.

"Very well," he said, again through his interpreter.

Quickly Reuben called for Judah, and the two men hastened toward the stable where their donkeys were tethered. When they returned, bearing bags full of choice products from Canaan, Joseph was deeply moved.

As the gifts of ointment, exotic nuts, and perfumes were spread upon a floor tarp, the Hebrew was poignantly reminded of his country and of his life in the shepherd hills.

Barely able to contain his feelings, he thanked the men and asked, "Is your old father well, of whom you spoke? Is he still alive?"

"Your servant, our father, is well," they replied, bowing down again in homage. If they wondered at the longing in the governor's tone, they were in no position to question it and kept their eyes to the ground.

"Please stand," he repeated. "Take your seats."

Through a haze of tears, he studied their faces, one by one, until he came to Benjamin.

"Is this your youngest brother?" he inquired, knowing very well that he was.

"Yes, sir," Reuben assured him. "You commanded us to bring him to you, and this we have done."

But Joseph was not concerned for Reuben's defense. His gaze was riveted to the son of Rachel, his only full brother.

"May God be gracious to you, my son," he said, his voice breaking.

Suddenly Joseph could bear the ache of his heart no longer, and turning about, left the dining room.

To the amazement of all who were present, both Hebrews and Egyptians, the governor disappeared into his chamber, weeping.

For a long while he was gone, until the company grew restless, and the servants and steward were perplexed as to what they should do.

But at last he emerged, having washed his face and gained control of himself.

"Serve the meal," he commanded.

Receiving no explanation, the servants and the guests followed his directive. Joseph was served at his private table, the Egyptian officials at theirs, and the guests at one long spread.

But before they were served, Joseph cleared his throat, looking unhappy with the arrangement.

"Put them in order of their ages," he commanded his steward.

When the poor fellow looked baffled, Joseph rose up and pointed to the brothers, one by one.

"This is the eldest," he said, indicating Reuben, "and this the second," to Judah.

From the firstborn, all the way down to Benjamin, he gave their rank with unfailing accuracy, adding mystery to mystery.

"How can he know?" Gad marveled.

"Quiet!" Naphtali whispered.

Obediently, the men took their designated places, looking at one another in astonishment.

When the meal began to be served, the governor still seemed dissatisfied.

Rising again from his seat, he carried platter after platter of delicacies from his own table to the table of the Israelites. And surprising everyone, he joined them.

"Here, son, have some more," he said, loading Benjamin's plate with a heap of food five times the size of his brothers'.

With a grin, Joseph began to drink with them, proposing toast after toast—to Canaan, to their father, to their welfare, to their donkeys, to anything he could name—until all were too merry to wonder, too merry to question, too merry to be mystified.

For now, they would set aside their fears. For now, they were free with the Egyptian who knew them better than they knew themselves.

# 44

It was the next morning before the Israelites, their caravan loaded with food and supplies, set out again for Canaan.

Their spirits heady with wine and a night full of partying, they were a lighthearted crew.

As the towers of Succoth grew smaller upon the retreating horizon, they felt free to discuss the events of the previous day.

But once again, they reached no credible conclusion regarding the prime minister's behavior. They would have written him off as an unpredictable lunatic, had it not been for his uncanny knowledge of their relative ranks and ages.

"Surely he is no madman," they concluded.

"Perhaps he is a wizard," someone suggested. "We have heard how he predicted this time of famine."

Still, this did not explain his odd treatment of their little band.

They had no reason to complain, however, and every reason to rejoice. Simeon was safely with them, no harm had befallen Benjamin, and their fears of retribution were assuaged.

The governor had seen to it that they were generously treated in the marketplace, and they had come away with enough food to see their tribe through several more months.

Not only this, but once again he had replaced their

money in their bags, not allowing them to pay a shekel for the goods.

It was not until they heard the rush of horses' hooves behind them that they grew apprehensive again.

Looking back toward the city, they saw that a forbidding group of riders pursued them, and as they came closer, they recognized the governor's steward in the lead.

"In the name of Zaphenath-paneah," he called after them, "stop in your tracks!"

Stunned, they waited on the desert highway. When the man reached them, they were speechless, for his troops leaped from their mounts and drew their swords.

"Why have you repaid evil for good?" the steward demanded.

When the Israelites only stared at him in perplexity, he commanded his men to search the train.

"The master's silver goblet has been stolen!" the steward shouted. "The one he uses for divination! You have done a great wrong in taking it!"

Judah was the first to find his voice.

"Good sir," he defended, "why does my lord speak such words as these? Far be it from your servants to do such a thing! Remember, the money which we found in our sacks we brought back to you from Canaan. How then could we steal silver or gold from your master's house?"

When the soldiers continued to search the train, Judah became even more adamant.

"You shall not find it, sir! Not with us!" he cried. "Why, if you should find it with one of us, he should be put to death! And the rest of us shall be your slaves!"

"Very well," the steward agreed. "But the one who has it shall be my slave, and the rest of you shall be innocent."

Livid, Simeon and Levi ran to the donkeys and unloaded their sacks. Each brother followed suit, and as they opened them, they laughed together, shaking their heads and cursing.

One by one, beginning with Reuben and proceeding in order of rank, the steward's men searched the bags.

Ten out of the eleven had been riffled with no sign of the cup. Only Benjamin's remained, and the elder brothers were already reloading their pack animals when a cry halted them.

"Here it is!" one of the soldiers announced. "In the bag of the youngest!"

Benjamin, his face scarlet, turned helplessly to his brothers. "I . . . I did not steal it!" he insisted.

"Then how does it come to be in your bag?" the steward growled.

Grasping the youngster by the arm, he pushed him toward one of his men.

"Bind him!" he commanded. "I have heard that Hebrews make good slaves."

# 45

The time of reckoning had come at last.

In fear and trembling the Israelites, the eleven sons of Jacob, were brought before the lord of Egypt.

Had they been able to share their thoughts at this moment, they would have found them remarkably similar. For every one of them, save Benjamin, bore the guilt of the past uppermost in his mind, and they all believed that the inscrutable puzzle of their time in Egypt had a direct relationship to their great and hidden sin.

How the cup had come to be in the sack of the only innocent brother, none of them could imagine. But that Zaphenath-paneah was a wizard, none of them doubted.

Surely he was an instrument of the supernatural. They felt this not only because of the knowledge he had of them, not only because the steward had said the stolen cup was used for divination, but also because the strange governor seemed capable of reading their innermost souls.

Again today, as they stood before him, they shriveled beneath his gaze, beneath the haunting torment of his eyes which stripped them of all confidence.

What magic he had to know them, they could not guess. Their theology allowed for no good power outside Jehovah, yet they did not sense that Zaphenath-paneah's gift was rooted in evil.

All this they would have discussed together, had they the chance. But they must keep silent, or they would surely not live to see tomorrow.

Before them now, upon his lofty porch, sat the prime minister, his arms outstretched along the arms of his throne, his face full of disapproval.

As one body, the Hebrews fell to the ground, prostrating themselves hopelessly.

For a long time, Joseph said nothing. When he did at last address them, it was in his most regal voice.

"What is this deed that you have done?" he demanded. "Do you not know that I am indeed a wizard?"

Quaking with resignation, Judah replied, "What can we say to my lord? How can we justify ourselves? God has discovered our iniquity. We are my lord's slaves, we and the one who had the cup."

But Joseph, feigning indignation, objected, "No, no! Far be it from me to do this. The one who had the cup shall be my slave, but as for you, return in peace to your father."

Now of course Joseph knew that this only turned the knife of their guilt more keenly. For among all of them, only Benjamin deserved to be spared.

Suddenly forgetting all propriety, Judah approached the throne, desperate to be heard. "Oh my lord," he pleaded, "may your servant please reach your heart? Do not be angry with me, for you are equal to Pharaoh!"

With this, he recounted their first conversation, reminding him of their father and his tender love for their youngest brother.

"My father told us that if we took Benjamin from him, and if harm befell the lad, we would bring the old man's gray hair down to the grave in sorrow!"

By now, Judah was on his knees, weaving to and fro, his hands clasped before him.

"If we return to our father and the lad is not with us, our father will surely die! Please, let me remain instead of the lad. I shall be your slave, but let Benjamin return with the others."

In that instant, as Joseph read Judah's despair—the agony and repentance of the very one who, years before, would have sold him into slavery—a strange thing happened.

At work within Joseph's heart was an exposing razor of memory, peeling away, ever so painfully, layer upon layer of time and resentment.

Yes, he had been here before. He had seen all of this before, not in vision, but in reality. The scene had involved different characters, but the circumstances had been the same. And as the recollection grew within him, he began to shiver.

He recalled the day his father, Jacob, had gone in fear and trembling to meet Esau. He remembered what it had felt like to see his strong Papa prostrate before the notorious hunter, the one who had sought for years to take vengeance on Jacob's selfish sin.

If anyone had the right to retribution, it was Esau. And if anyone had the right to revenge, it was Joseph.

Suddenly, the prime minister, the great lord of Egypt, could control himself no longer.

Turning to his steward, barely able to see for the tears in his eyes, he cried, "Clear the court! Send everyone away!"

Once again, the steward was faced with the conundrum of his master's behavior. But compliantly he obeyed, clapping his hands and ushering all the servants and officials away from the porch, until the governor was left alone with the Israelites.

As he stood solitary before his brothers, he began to weep so loudly that all those who occupied his compound heard him. And between convulsive sobs he revealed himself.

"I am Joseph!" he cried in his native tongue. "Is my father still alive?"

Confounded silence choked the Hebrews, and they looked upon him as though not hearing.

"Please..." Joseph pleaded, holding out his hands, "come closer to me."

As they found strength to obey, Joseph removed his striped headdress so that he might look more familiar.

"I am your brother, Joseph, whom you sold into Egypt!" he declared.

As the men tried to absorb what he was saying, a hundred questions resisted it.

Joseph? Here in Egypt? They had nearly convinced themselves, after all this time, that their brother must be dead.

But, yes—he did look somewhat like the youngster they had left in the pit, like the ghost who had haunted their dreams all these years.

Yet, how had they "sold" him? And how had he come to this high station?

They were barely beginning to accept his identity when he spoke again.

"Do not be grieved or angry with yourselves because you sold me here. For God sent me before you to preserve life... to preserve you as a remnant in the earth and to keep you alive by a great deliverance."

Still the men were speechless. As Joseph read their mystified expressions, he went on.

"Now, therefore, although you left me for dead, so that I was picked up and sold, it was not you who sent me here, but God. He has made me a guide to Pharaoh, lord of all his household, and ruler over all the land of Egypt!"

By now he was pacing before them, his arms wide. "Hurry and go to my father. Tell him what God has done. Then return with him! Do not delay! You shall live in the land of Goshen, the finest shepherd land in Egypt! And you shall be near me, you and your children and your children's children and your flocks and your herds and all that you have!"

Someone in the group began to weep, and another to

laugh. Soon the entire company was giddy with the revelation.

"There now!" Joseph cried. "Your eyes see, and the eyes of my brother Benjamin see, that it is my mouth which is speaking to you!"

He stood now directly before the youngest son, studying the lavender lights in his eyes.

"Oh," he laughed, "I could not let you go! It was I who put the cup within your sack! Anything to stop you, to bring you back to me!"

Benjamin smiled broadly, and with sudden ecstasy Joseph fell on his neck, kissing him and weeping with him.

One by one he drew his awestruck brothers to him, embracing them and kissing them:

Reuben, who had been helpless to save him; Judah, who would have sold him; Simeon and Levi, who had been lions in his life; Gad and Asher, who would have killed him . . .

One by one by one . . .

And they marveled, overcome and grateful, just as Jacob had marveled when Esau lifted him from the dirt and forgave him.

# EPILOGUE

*There is a friend who sticks closer
than a brother.*

Proverbs 18:24b NASB

# Epilogue

# Epilogue

Jacob sat upon a broad plush seat in the golden chariot of his son, the prime minister of Egypt. On either side of him were two young boys, looking much like his beloved Rachel.

Manasseh and Ephraim studied the patriarch's aged face with awe. All their lives they had heard of Israel and his great faith. But to actually sit in his presence brought them closer to the legends, closer to their father's God.

Jacob wrapped an arm around each of them, his eyes wistful and bright as he watched the passing terrain.

Joseph, who sat across from him, his lovely wife at his side, breathed softly into her ear. "That is my father, Asenath. My father, here with us!"

"Yes," she whispered, her lips parting in a smile.

She had never known her husband to be so happy, so fulfilled, and her heart glowed with joy.

The family had just taken the old patriarch to meet Pharaoh in Avaris, the king's Delta palace, and were now returning him to Goshen, where the mighty tribe of Israel was settling in.

It had been a hard thing for Jacob to leave Canaan, to come to a new land where shepherds were still often held in disdain.

But Joseph had chosen a choice site for their settlement, a fertile valley much like the Vale of Shechem and studded with oaks like Mamre.

As the chariot, driven by a court chauffeur, came

within view of the vast property, Jacob breathed deeply of the country breeze.

Warm air currents perpetually wafted over this place, passing across miles of undulating green like a caress. They bore a hint of the cooling sea as they descended from the north, and they blended with the heat of the eastern desert, creating a perfect climate.

So lush was the land of Goshen that it was also named for Raamses, one of the most renowned of the Pharaohs. This had been his favorite place, he who owned the world.

Joseph would never forget the sight of his frail father, dressed in simple nomad's robes, as he stood before the present king of Egypt. This Pharaoh, still very proud of his own shepherd roots, had welcomed him eagerly. And they had talked for a long time.

"How old are you?" the young king had asked, entranced by Jacob's wise face.

"The years of my sojourning are 130," Jacob had replied. "Few and unpleasant have been the years of my life, nor have I attained the years that my fathers lived during the days of their sojourning."

So moved had Salatis been by the venerable elder's quiet spirit, that he had actually stepped down from his throne to speak further with him.

"And your God is the God of the desert?"

"The God of the whole earth, the sea, the sky, and all that is in them," Jacob had answered.

It was easy to see that Pharaoh was touched by this. When he drew even nearer to the old man, raising Jacob's wizened hands in his own, the whole court had been breathless.

"Bless me, Father," he had said.

And so Jacob had complied, resting his hands on the young king's head and calling down the strength of Jehovah on his reign.

As the chariot traveled toward the Goshen settlement, Jacob appeared to be at peace. Joseph lifted Asenath's hand to his lips, praying privately that the old man's remaining years would be happy.

Somehow, seeing the light on Jacob's face as they pulled into camp, he knew they would be.

* * *

Joseph would return to the Avaris court in the morning. For tonight he wished to walk through Goshen Vale, to see that all was well with his father's people.

He had left Asenath and her sons with the women of the camp, and had walked some distance, marveling at the size of the tribe. Hundreds of souls were numbered among it—sons and their wives, children and grandchildren, menservants and womenservants. And despite the famine, it was a wealthy company.

As Joseph passed through the settlement, he was greeted warmly by all, and was at last hailed by one of his favorites.

Eagerly Reuben joined him, his handsome face beaming. "May I walk a little way with you?" he called.

"Please," Joseph greeted. "I would like that."

Always the younger brother had admired Jacob's firstborn. And now more than ever, he was proud to be kin to the striking Reuben.

"Judah has told me that you alone, of all my brothers, tried to rescue me from the pit," Joseph said. "You always were my savior," he confessed, "from the time I was small."

Reuben smiled, remembering the lad's many tussles with Simeon, Levi, and the others.

"You had a hard way to go, Little One," he recalled.

Joseph laughed aloud. "It has been some time since I was called that!"

Suddenly Reuben blushed, hoping he had not offended. After all, this was the prime minister of Egypt to whom he spoke!

But Joseph clapped him on the back, and Reuben sighed.

"The men have been talking to me," the elder said. "They are still somewhat afraid."

"Why?" Joseph marveled. "Have I not done well by them?"

"Indeed," Reuben asserted. "But I suppose they find it hard to receive such forgiveness. They fear that you have done it for Jacob's sake, and that when our father passes on . . ."

Joseph stopped in the path and looked deep into his brother's eyes.

"Tell them, for me, not to be afraid. Am I in God's place? They may have meant evil against me, but God has turned it for good, in order to bring about this present result . . . to preserve many people."

Reuben listened in amazement, and would have objected, but could not.

"Tell them not to fear," Joseph repeated.

The elder bowed his head, his heart too full to speak, and with a nod he turned to leave.

When Joseph was alone again, he ventured to the edge of camp. Taking a seat on the rise of a little hill, he looked back over the great company and the circles of firelight which marked it against the earth.

The sun had fully set now, and night had fallen. Through Joseph's mind passed countless faces, many as familiar as his own childhood, and others whom he had never seen until this day—the faces of his father's people.

Closing his eyes, he drew his knees to his chest and recalled, as though it had never gone, his youth in the shepherd hills. For the first time in years, he communed with his God in the quiet of the wilderness.

When a shadow passed between himself and the moon above, he opened his eyes again and saw before him yet one more face.

"Papa," he sighed, "how good of you to join me!"

Stooping down, Jacob sat with him, his snowy beard gracing his lap.

"You were a good wrestler," the old Hebrew said.

"I did not let the Lord go easily," Joseph replied.

"You did not let him go until he blessed you!" the patriarch laughed.

For a long while, the two sat together—Joseph and his Papa, his mentor of the faith.

Tonight the past and the present were in harmony, and all the dreams Joseph had ever dreamed had come true.

# HARVEST HOUSE PUBLISHERS
For The Best In Inspirational Fiction

## RUTH LIVINGSTON HILL CLASSICS

Bright Conquest
The Homecoming
The Jeweled Sword

Morning Is For Joy
This Side of Tomorrow
The South Wind Blew Softly

## *June Masters Bacher*
## PIONEER ROMANCE NOVELS

**Series 1**
1. Love Is a Gentle Stranger
2. Love's Silent Song

3. Diary of a Loving Heart
4. Love Leads Home

**Series 2**
1. Journey To Love
2. Dreams Beyond Tomorrow

3. Seasons of Love
4. My Heart's Desire

**Series 3**
1. Love's Soft Whisper
2. Love's Beautiful Dream
3. When Hearts Awaken

4. Another Spring
5. When Morning Comes
   Again

## MYSTERY/ROMANCE NOVELS

Echoes From the Past, *Bacher*
Mist Over Morro Bay, *Page/Fell*
Secret of the East Wind, *Page/Fell*
Storm Clouds Over Paradise, *Page/Fell*
Beyond the Windswept Sea, *Page/Fell*
The Legacy of Lillian Parker, *Holden*
The Compton Connection, *Holden*
The Caribbean Conspiracy, *Holden*
The Gift, *Hensley/Miller*

## PIONEER ROMANCE NOVELS

Sweetbriar, *Wilbee*
The Sweetbriar Bride, *Wilbee*
The Tender Summer, *Johnson*

## BIBLICAL NOVELS

Esther, *Traylor*

Available at your local Christian bookstore

Dear Reader:

We would appreciate hearing from you regarding this Harvest House fiction book. It will enable us to continue to give you the best in Christian publishing.

1. What most influenced you to purchase *Joseph*?
   - ☐ Author
   - ☐ Subject matter
   - ☐ Backcover copy
   - ☐ Recommendations
   - ☐ Cover/Title
   - ☐ _____

2. Where did you purchase this book?
   - ☐ Christian bookstore
   - ☐ General bookstore
   - ☐ Department store
   - ☐ Grocery store
   - ☐ Other

3. Your overall rating of this book:
   ☐ Excellent  ☐ Very good  ☐ Good  ☐ Fair  ☐ Poor

4. How likely would you be to purchase other books by this author?
   - ☐ Very likely
   - ☐ Somewhat likely
   - ☐ Not very likely
   - ☐ Not at all

5. What types of books most interest you?
   (check all that apply)
   - ☐ Women's Books
   - ☐ Marriage Books
   - ☐ Current Issues
   - ☐ Self Help/Psychology
   - ☐ Bible Studies
   - ☐ Fiction
   - ☐ Biographies
   - ☐ Children's Books
   - ☐ Youth Books
   - ☐ Other _____

6. Please check the box next to your age group.
   - ☐ Under 18
   - ☐ 18-24
   - ☐ 25-34
   - ☐ 35-44
   - ☐ 45-54
   - ☐ 55 and over

**Mail to:** Editorial Director
Harvest House Publishers
1075 Arrowsmith
Eugene, OR 97402

Name _____

Address _____

City _____ State _____ Zip _____

**Thank you for helping us to help you in future publications!**